They All Need to Talk

Wilma M. Possien
University of South Alabama

They All Need to Talk

oral communication in the language arts program

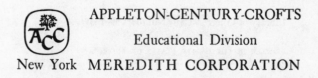

APPLETON-CENTURY-CROFTS

Educational Division

New York MEREDITH CORPORATION

To Mark and Lawrence,
whose oral development provided the inspiration

Library of Congress Card Number: 69-15371

PRINTED IN THE UNITED STATES OF AMERICA
390-71385-6

preface

The language arts in the elementary school are usually regarded as a complex of the skills and understandings involved in listening, speaking, writing, and reading. These four major aspects encompass a multitude of related abilities—handwriting, spelling, personal and practical writing, grammar, punctuation, word recognition, and sentence and paragraph construction, to mention but a few.

As might be expected, such a complicated field has challenged the study and research of many capable educators and has demanded the intensive effort and attention of many classroom teachers. In spite of our best efforts, inadequacies in language usage continue to plague teachers and to hinder the progress of learners at all levels of education.

Years of experience as a classroom teacher, as an elementary-school principal, and, more recently, as a college teacher involved in teacher preparation have convinced this writer that a fundamental cause of difficulties with language usage is the lack of provision for the development of oral language skills at the elementary-school level. Some children never learn to express their ideas because they have neither the opportunities nor the tools for effective oral communication. They are expected to use language in writing and reading long before they have had experiences that would help them develop concepts of its symbolic nature and communicative function. They are asked to read before they are capable of coping with abstract thought and to write before they have anything to say.

Most of the language arts textbooks used in teacher education and by practicing teachers attempt to deal with the total spectrum of language abilities. I feel that teachers would welcome supplementary materials which provide greater depth of consideration than these and more specificity of help in one particular aspect of language development.

This book, then, was planned around two major purposes. The first is to help teachers develop an understanding of the fundamental importance of oral communication in a highly articulate world society. The second is to provide specific teaching situations, with appropriate techniques and procedures, designed to give children a wide range of stimulating, meaningful experiences in the development of oral language skills.

No such project could be completed without the help and encouragement of many people. The author is deeply indebted to Dr. J. Howe Hadley, Dean of the College of Education of the University of South Alabama, whose philosophy of administration allows academic freedom and encourages creative thought, and to two colleagues, Dr. Mary Jo Harris and Dr. Wayne Scrivner, who offered valuable suggestions and many practical helps. Teachers and children in many classrooms have provided many ideas and anecdotes. Specific mention must be made of Mrs. Kathleen Parker, Mrs. Aileen Cole, Mrs. Dorothy Schwartz, and Sister Thaddeus, whose skillful, creative work with children is described or transcribed in the book. The laborious, mechanical chores of typing and proofreading were handled cheerfully and efficiently by Mrs. Georgia Self, Mrs. Jean Blanchard, and Mrs. Lamona Lucas.

The entire process and all of the interpersonal relationships involved have been characterized by the author's wish for all readers of the book and for all the children they teach:

Happy Talking!

W. M. P.

contents

one

The rationale

guidelines for action

Traditionally, the people of the United States have entrusted to the educational institution much of the task of acculturating the young. They have expected the schools to achieve a commonality of learning and to instill values and standards held acceptable by the culture. In turn, those who have been responsible for the operation of the schools have worked to identify the specific cultural expectations and to develop the means of implementing them. Prolonged and bitter controversy has marked these efforts in such matters as curriculum content, teacher preparation, teaching methodology, and school finance. Such divergence of opinion has not, however, been characteristic of efforts to identify educational objectives.

Throughout the twentieth century, as educators have worked to carry out the great American experiment of educating all of the children of all its people, there has been a surprising degree of unanimity among those charged with the task of establishing the basic purposes of education. Major social problems and societal needs have caused close examination of the aims and functions of public education. The results of these examinations have had significant effects on the development of the educational process.

The general objectives of education

The concern over the large number of young men rejected for military service in World War I brought about one of the most

1

widely acclaimed and influential statements of educational objectives. In 1918 the famous Seven Cardinal Principles were published by the Commission on the Reorganization of Secondary Education. The commission's report included these objectives: [1]

1. Good health.
2. Command of fundamental processes.
3. Worthy home membership.
4. Vocation.
5. Citizenship.
6. Worthy use of leisure time.
7. Ethical character.

In the mid-1930's America was just recovering from the impact of a major economic depression, and another major world crisis was brewing. The National Education Association, concerned about the needs and pressures brought on youth by the acceleration of industrialization and by troubled international relationships, appointed a second commission to study the problem of identification of educational objectives. The work of this group, the Educational Policies Commission, resulted in the publication of the highly significant *Purposes of Education in American Democracy,* which listed the four major aims of education as: [2]

1. Self-realization.
2. The formation of good human relationships.
3. Economic efficiency.
4. Civic responsibility.

Toward the close of World War II, faced with the gigantic task of helping to bring order out of chaos, educators again felt the need for a careful consideration of basic guidelines for educational efforts. Two groups published very influential lists of educational aims. The first of these was included in a publication of the Educational Poli-

[1] Commission on the Reorganization of Secondary Education, *Cardinal Principles of Education,* U.S. Office of Education Bulletin No. 35 (Washington, D.C.: Government Printing Office, 1918), pp. 10–11.
[2] Educational Policies Commission, *The Purposes of Education in American Democracy* (Washington, D.C.: National Education Association, 1935).

cies Commission in 1944 and has been widely quoted as "The Ten Imperative Needs of Youth":

1. All youth need to develop salable skills and those understandings and attitudes that make the worker an intelligent and productive participant in economic life. To this end, most youth need supervised work experience as well as education in the skills and knowledge of their occupations.

2. All youth need to develop and maintain good health and physical fitness.

3. All youth need to understand the rights and duties of the citizen of a democratic society, and to be diligent and competent in the performance of their obligations as members of the community and citizens of the state and nation.

4. All youth need to understand the significance of the family for the individual and society and the conditions conducive to successful family life.

5. All youth need to know how to purchase and use goods and services intelligently, understanding both the values received by the consumer and the economic consquences of their acts.

6. All youth need to understand the methods of science, the influence of science on human life, and the main scientific facts concerning the nature of the world and of men.

7. All youth need opportunities to develop their capacities to appreciate beauty, in literature, art, music, and nature.

8. All youth need to be able to use their leisure time well and to budget it wisely, balancing activities that yield satisfactions to the individual with those that are socially useful.

9. All youth need to develop respect for other persons, to grow in their insight into ethical values and principles, and to be able to live and work cooperatively with others.

10. All youth need to grow in ability, to think rationally, to express their thoughts clearly, and to read and listen with understanding.[3]

The second set was the work of the Harvard Committee, whose recommendations were published in 1945. That significant report stressed the fact that education must be concerned with the prepara-

[3] Educational Policies Commission, *Education for All American Youth* (Washington, D.C.: National Education Association, 1944), pp. 225–226.

tion for life of the whole being, and it singled out these four qualities of mind as being of ultimate importance: [4]

1. Effective thinking.
2. Communication.
3. Ability to make relative judgments.
4. Discretion between values.

The decade of the 1950's was marked by internal turmoil and external strife. Changes in major social institutions, international unrest, and the vociferous charges of critics of American education prompted President Eisenhower, in 1955, to call the historic White House Conference on Education. That group of 2,000 citizens, predominantly made up of laymen but including prominent educators from all levels and fields of education, gave careful consideration to the major problems facing education. Its conclusions, representing a consensus of the group's members, called for a fourteen-point focus of educational efforts:

1. The fundamental skills of communication—reading, writing, spelling, as well as other elements of effective oral and written expression; the arithmetical and mathematical skills, including problem solving. While schools are doing the best job in their history in teaching these skills, continuous improvement is desirable and necessary.

2. Appreciation of our democratic heritage.

3. Knowledge of civic rights and responsibilities and of American institutions.

4. Respect and appreciation for human values and for the beliefs of others.

5. Ability to think and evaluate constructively and creatively.

6. Effective work habits and self-discipline.

7. Social competency as a contributing member of the family and the community.

8. Ethical behavior based on a sense of moral and spiritual values.

9. Intellectual curiosity and eagerness for life-long learning.

10. Esthetic appreciation and self-expression in the arts.

11. Physical and mental health.

12. Wise use of time, including constructive leisure pursuits.

[4] Report of the Harvard Committee, *General Education in a Free Society* (Cambridge, Mass.: Harvard University Press, 1945).

13. Understanding of the physical world and man's relation to it as represented through basic knowledge of the sciences.

14. An awareness of our relationships with the world community.[5]

The 1960's have not lacked attention to educational objectives. The explosion of new insights concerning the multidimensional structure of human ability and the modifiability of the intelligence quotient, or I.Q., the recent developments in learning theory, and the current emphasis on the effects of language deprivation have resulted in a spate of worthwhile attempts to identify defensible educational purposes. The resultant guidelines are geared toward members of a society which is characterized by rapid and unpredictable change. Because of increased knowledge of the vast complexity of human behavior and of modern society, the new stated aims are, without fail, less prescriptive but more challenging, less specific but more comprehensive, less definite but more demanding. In short, modern statements of objectives do not depart radically from earlier lists in looking at the needs of the end product of education—i.e., the learner; they differ chiefly in viewing the processes of education. Glen Heathers gives a thoughtful summary which is characteristic of modern statements. He writes:

The views of today's reform spokesmen about the aims of education emphasize five great themes or purposes. These are:

1. Stress the teaching of theory rather than information within the content areas of the curriculum.

2. Stress the process goals of education to ensure that every student becomes a competent learner.

3. Establish excellence as the criterion of accomplishment with all students at all levels of instruction.

4. Find ways to individualize instruction to meet the learning needs and readiness of each student.

5. Develop programs that equalize educational opportunity through offering every student access to a first-rate school and through providing compensatory education for underprivileged children and youths.

These purposes are not new in education; however, the degree of

[5] The Reports of the White House Conference on Education (Washington, D.C.: Government Printing Office, 1955).

emphasis being placed on them is new, and many approaches to accomplishing them are new.[6]

A survey of the foregoing statements points up the commonality of thought underlying the general objectives of American education. Certain variables are inherent in all the lists. These include the learner operating effectively as an autonomous individual and as a participating member of his social matrix. More important to the immediate purposes of this book, there is, in each instance, an explicit statement or an implied position which stresses the importance of the development of the communication skills.

Objectives in the language arts

A similar survey of the literature in the language arts field makes apparent a second area of consensus. Nowhere in the reams of materials which have been published can the reader find mention of the antiquated and stereotyped concept of teaching "English" as an isolated and separate "subject." This terminology connotes a set formula of rules to be memorized and proved in use or an equation involving preordained syntactical structure. Instead, the orientation is toward the organization of areas of study called the language arts, the emphasis is on the development of a constellation of skills aimed at effective communication, and the basic purpose is to increase the learner's power of language usage.

"Scholars in the field of linguistics," writes Ruth Strickland, "are concerned with the science of language and with comparisons between languages. Teachers and parents are interested chiefly in the functions of language, its development by children, and its effects upon their lives and personalities." [7]

Shane and his associates identify the areas included in this functional approach when they write:

The four components of communication are taught in the elementary school as the language arts. The term language arts is used to designate

[6] Glen Heathers, "Influencing Change at the Elementary Level," in Richard I. Miller (ed.) *Perspectives on Educational Change* (New York: Appleton-Century-Crofts, 1967), p. 24.

[7] Ruth G. Strickland, *The Language Arts in the Elementary School* (Boston: D. C. Heath and Company, 1957), p. 15.

the fusion of many language skills into one broad field in which the related phases of expressive and receptive communication are taught in *relationship*. As a general rule, the language arts include reading, creative writing and creative expression, handwriting skills, children's literature, spelling, grammar and usage, listening, vocabulary building, and, in some schools, instruction in a second language.[8]

This approach is based on several significant premises which are basic to an adequate understanding of the importance of the language arts, of their place in the curriculum, and of the methodology most effective in their development.

1. The ability to use language is the unique quality of humanness. Language is the tool which enables the child to know what he is, who he is, who others are, and how and why their lives affect his. Through the process of communication he comes to regard himself as a worthy member of his family and community or as an inadequate, unwanted individual, and, by the same process, the world becomes a friendly, accepting environment or a forbidding, hostile prison.

2. For better or for worse, regardless of what the school does, the child will learn some means of communication. From the time of his first vocalized sound, his language power increases at an astronomical rate until, when he enters school, he brings with him such a wealth of learning about language that he will never again be able to learn as much in a like period of time.

3. The school's job, then, is to refine, to expand, and to enrich the language skills already developed and to use these to build those skills whose acquisition involves direct instruction. Such skills as reading and writing are based on the ability to use abstract symbols and generally must be taught.

4. The world of today is dominated and saturated by symbols. The learner's ability to cope effectively with the sophisticated symbolization of the mass media will determine, to a large extent, his attitudes, his values, his use of time, and his consumption of the world's goods.

5. Further, the accumulated heritage of civilization is trans-

[8] Harold G. Shane, June Grant Mulry, Mary E. Reddin, and Margaret C. Gillispie, *Improving Language Arts Instruction in the Elementary School* (Columbus, Ohio: Charles E. Merrill Books, Inc., 1962), p. 12.

mitted through the symbols of communication. This means that efficiency in the language skills is prerequisite to academic achievement and to success in any area of endeavor.

6. Instruction in the language arts, then, begins the day a child enters school and ends the day he leaves. It is a continuing responsibility which cuts across all the school day's activities and cannot be restricted to a "language period." Language usage is the tool which is improved by challenging opportunities for use and sharpened by the teaching skills of a sensitive, perceptive teacher.

Objectives of oral communication

This author takes the position that the skills of oral communication are prerequisite to the development of all language skills. Indeed, there appears to be unanimous agreement that the specific communication skill which is most critical for the fully functioning individual in modern society and for success in any academic area is proficiency in the use of oral language. Wilmer K. Trauger devotes the third chapter of *Language Arts in the Elementary School* to oral communication. He writes that speech is a type of language expression that is swift, complicated, frequent, and primary. "Children, in school and out," he writes, "maintain a perpetual flow of talk and gesture. A teacher's problem is less one of finding opportunities for children to speak or listen than of discovering how to use the abundant occasions wisely." [9]

The editors of *Readings in the Language Arts* introduce the papers on listening and speaking with this statement:

> The ability to use the spoken word to accurately communicate thought or express feeling is the most significant skill developed by individuals in the highly complex social organization of modern life.[10]

[9] Wilmer K. Trauger, *Language Arts in the Elementary School* (New York: McGraw-Hill Book Company, Inc., 1963), p. 27.

[10] Verna Diechman Anderson, Paul S. Anderson, Francis Ballantine, and Virgil M. Howes (eds.), *Readings in the Language Arts* (New York: The Macmillan Company, 1964), p. 45.

As Shane and his associates tell us,

> [A] major responsibility of the teacher is helping children develop and increase the skill and fluidity that characterize language facility. We know that children come to school knowing how to talk, but we sometimes forget that they will go right on learning how to talk, either effectively or ineffectively, well into their adult years. Children must know how to express their thoughts to others and, in turn, they must be able to gather critical information from others.[11]

This point is well taken. A colleague of mine tells his students that we constantly underestimate the learner's ability and overestimate his experiences. James C. MacCampbell agrees with this need to examine our assumptions when he writes:

> Probably teachers have always agreed in theory that the skills of oral language are basic to those of reading and writing. Yet until fairly recently, they have been slow to recognize that oral skills themselves are worthy of organized classroom instruction. This may be largely due to the very fact that speech is so integral to every personality and so much more commonly used than the written word.[12]

The present situation

It is apparent that a wide discrepancy exists between the recommended philosophy and procedures for language instruction and the actual practices in classrooms. In essence, the implication of all stated purposes of education and of instruction in the language arts is that we should strive for learners who are proficient in oral communication. What we actually *do* seems quite different. In many classrooms throughout the country the order of business in the language arts is restricted to the completion of endless "fill-in-the-blank" exercises within a scheduled period of time and to the writing of countless paragraphs or themes.

11 Harold G. Shane et al., *op. cit.*, p. 22.
12 James C. MacCampbell, *Readings in the Language Arts in the Elementary School* (Boston: D. C. Heath and Company, 1964), p. 123.

For far too long teachers have given lip service to the concept of fusing language instruction with the ongoing instructional program, of making language development an integral function of the development of the "whole child." Lip service in the form of verbalized clichés accomplishes nothing. Frost makes this point clear:

The interrelationships that exist between language, intelligence, thinking, and social, physical, and emotional factors imply that the effective language arts program will have as its focus the "whole child." Although this "holistic" concept has maintained theoretical consideration for many years, practical application has lagged. As a consequence, more attention is commonly given to what is "taught" than to how learning occurs. This results in superficial learner commitment and shallow thinking. The child—expected to adjust his needs to the school's goals, modify his goals to grade-level standards, and gear his thinking toward accumulation of facts—has limited opportunity for growth in language power.[13]

Our programs would appear to be based on two assumptions: first, that written communication is more important than and precedes oral communication and, second, that people learn to *speak* by *writing*.

The results of a program based on such erroneous assumptions are too well known to require documentation; elementary-school children who are bored and frustrated, high-school students who "hate English," college students who are unable to present a coherent oral report, and adults who freeze at the prospect of expressing an opinion at the P.T.A. meeting seem to be the rule rather than the exception.

It is to those teachers who would like to do something about these attitudes and needs that the information and suggestions in this book are addressed. The first part of chapter two attempts to present and analyze some recent developments concerning learning and intelligence which seem to have great significance for understanding language development. The final section of that chapter explores some major deterrents to the development of facility in

---

[13] Joe L. Frost, "Language Development in Children," in Joe L. Frost (ed.), *Issues and Innovations in the Teaching of Reading* (Chicago: Scott, Foresman and Company, 1967), pp. 7–8.

oral language and makes suggestions aimed at the elimination of such impeding factors.

Chapter three deals with the building blocks of oral communication. *Words* may be the prosaic, flimsy sticks used by that well-known "first little pig" to build his shabby, flimsy house, or they may be the rich mortar and substantial bricks used by the third one to build his attractive, sturdy dwelling. *Words, words, words!* is the subtitle of the third chapter, and the means of developing rich, colorful, precise vocabulary is its content.

Each of the subsequent chapters deals with one specific technique for use in developing the program in oral communication and offers suggested activities which may be helpful to in-service and preservice teachers. Chapter four presents the case for the inclusion of creative dramatics in the elementary-school program and points out ways to use this technique. Perhaps the most frequently used, and misused, technique of oral expression is that of discussion. Chapter five, subtitled *let's talk it over,* begins with a depth definition of what discussion really is and continues with guidelines for the development of effective classroom discussion. Reporting is frequently a deadly, monotonous presentation of plagiarized material, but it can be a significant learning experience. Chapter six takes up the means of developing good reports in the elementary school. Children's books can be fascinating and challenging. Using these beautiful books in the development of language skills is the topic of chapter seven. Chapter eight, subtitled *world of words—and wonder,* deals with the use of poetry. Enjoyment of poetry can add tremendously to the richness of life. The concluding chapter, chapter nine outlines a position on the evaluation of progress in language development and presents specific suggestions to help teachers with this difficult task. It is an appropriate final topic for a book aimed at the development of more effective oral communication.

two

More rationale

breaking the lockstep

The present time is an exciting one to be involved in the educative endeavor, and future decades promise to be quite as challenging. Much of the impact of the "knowledge explosion" has been on the field of education. More is known now about the learner and the learning process than ever before. More educational thought and research have been devoted to studies of human learning and human variability than to any other field in education. This has resulted in a proliferation of knowledge which is truly amazing.

The fruition of these efforts in terms of increased teaching effectiveness seems, however, to be a slow process. The traditional lag between the time something is discovered about the educative process and the time that knowledge is put to use in the classrooms of America has been estimated at twenty to fifty years. This lag must not be allowed to persist. If teaching procedures do not keep pace with new knowledge, the teaching profession will forfeit its position of educational leadership and could well become a mechanized agent for automated education.

The effectiveness of any educational practice must be evaluated in terms of how much and what kinds of learning it produces. It follows, then, that the first step in eliminating the gap between knowledge and practice is the acquisition of some basic understanding of learning—what it is, how it occurs, and how it may be facilitated or impeded. The psychology of learning is a complex and difficult field, so only those characteristics of learning which have obvious implications for the development of oral language skills are discussed here.

Characteristics of learning

First consideration must be given to the premise that learning is a *personal* matter. When an individual feels that previous responses or reactions are inadequate in a new situation, he modifies or changes his previous behavior. He *learns*—facts, attitudes, skills, or values. Two key factors operate here. The learner must recognize a problem, a need to change previously learned behavior, and he must see some factor in the learning situation as potentially helpful to him in solving his problem. Learning then becomes a matter of individual perception. Arthur W. Combs writes:

> Perceptual psychology now tells us that how a person behaves is a function of his perceptions. Effective, efficient behavior, therefore, will depend upon the nature of the individual's perceptual field.[1]

Education has not been negligent in the matter of gathering information and making it available to students. Nor has it failed in the identification of defensible purposes and goals. The difficulties lie in making the information assume personal meaning for the learner and in structuring the knowledge in such a manner that the individual perceives it as important to the accomplishment of his purposes.

So the ultimate choice of what will be learned is made by the learner. Consciously or unconsciously he rejects those learning tasks which lack meaning or clarity, and he willingly attacks those which seem significant. It is the task of the teacher to asssess his needs and to set up learning conditions which enable him to achieve his self-determined goals. According to Alexander Frazier,

We are finding that, when the individual is psychologically and meth-

---

[1] Arthur W. Combs, "Personality Theory and Its Implications for Curriculum Development," in Alexander Frazier (ed.), *Learning More About Learning* (Washington, D.C.: Association for Supervision and Curriculum Development, 1959), p. 13.

odologically free to do so, he chooses to learn much more than he has to. Our role is not so much to lay out the amount to be learned as to arrange for the learner to make use of whatever he can that promises to help him make increasing sense out of his world.[2]

Even a cursory observation of children's behavior will reveal the child's awareness of his need to communicate. He strives mightily to express his desires, his excitement, and his information. If we give him many, varied opportunities to speak and to develop a rich store of the tools for speaking, we may be sure that his language power will increase as his perceptual framework grows.

The need for a variety of opportunities suggests a second characteristic of learning: It thrives on *novelty*. Ask anyone to describe his favorite teacher; inevitably the responses will include some mention of participating in novel, stimulating, fresh learning activities. "She made things interesting." "I'll never forget the trip we made to collect specimens of sea life." "We worked like dogs on that debate, but it was fun." "She livened up every lesson with her great sense of humor." These comments each describe an imaginative teacher who made learning its own reinforcing agent by using a variety of teaching techniques. William Kessen puts it this way:

Many of the reevaluations of thinking put the relation between the structure of the person and the structure of the environment in the center of theoretical consideration. The properties of external stimulation that are seen as critical with respect to intrinsic sources of change are those that are customarily covered by such words as "novelty", "change", surprisingness", "complexity", "congruity", "ambiguity" and "lack of clarity." . . . Whatever the theoretical underlay, evidence has begun to accumulate that skillful variation of environmental uncertainty can increase retention, understanding, transfer to new situations, recognition of problem solutions when achieved, and the tendency of the child to search for information![3]

Hopefully, no child in future decades will be subjected to what has been called "two by four" teaching—teaching limited to

2 Alexander Frazier, "Needed: A New Vocabulary for Individual Difference," in Maurie Hillson (ed.), *Change and Innovation in Elementary School Organization* (New York: Holt, Rinehart and Winston, Inc., 1965), p. 27.

3 William Kessen, "The Strategy of Instruction," in *Learning About Learning* (Washington, D.C.: Bureau of Research, U.S. Office of Education, 1964), p. 99.

the two covers of the book and the four walls of the room. Monotony and boredom are antithetical to learning. Children do not gain greater fluency in language usage by filling in blanks or diagramming sentences. The desired gains can occur only when children are stimulated by novel, challenging situations which arouse their interest and make the acquisition of language power important to them as individual learners.

This points to a third dimension of learning. It is always *multiple*. Frequently, the concomitant learnings which grow out of a specific learning task are more pervasive than the ones the teacher has sought to instill. Can the reader recall the hours spent on the "correct" use of *can* and *may* or *shall* and *will* during his elementary-school days? It is possible that most of us can verbalize the rules for the use of these words. It is highly probable that we learned some other things which our well-meaning teachers never considered. Vivid recollections of her own attitudes and of the comments of classmates indicate to this writer that, as we learned to use *can* and *may* correctly (maybe), we also learned that school is a place set aside from life, dealing with little ticky-tacky problems which aren't very important anyway; that verbalism is the thing— if you can *say* the rule, you're assured of a good grade; that concentration and attentiveness aren't important—you can fill in these blanks without half thinking about them; and that handwriting isn't important, either—she never even looks at these workbooks . . . so "I'm gonna call Mom and ask if I *can* go to June's house this afternoon."

Since it is apparent that learning does not operate on a simple basis of one thing at a time, it is important that each learning task be evaluated in terms of possible concomitant learnings of attitudes, values, habits, and skills. For it is these which determine the learner's commitment to learning, the transfer value of the task, and the individual's perception of the learning situation.

The final characteristic of learning to be considered for the purposes of this book is that it is *symbol-based*. Man's unique ability to symbolize gives him the ability to engage in abstract thought, and all of the higher level thought processes require this ability. Irving E. Sigel writes:

Language provides the individual with a set of labels which refer to parts or to wholes, to attributes or to the total. The acquisition of the labels is a function of the individual's sociocultural experiences. The labels acquired enable him to identify and communicate about his environment.[4]

The need for labels puts a peculiar responsibility on the language arts program. In the first place, many children come to school from homes which lack adequate objects to label and sufficient experiences in attaching labels. These sociocultural factors preclude the child's identification with and communication about his world. Such youngsters are alienated from the school society and from the process of learning by their inability to communicate.

Whatever else we know about learning, it is mandatory that we realize that learning requires some highly generalized intellectual skills. One of these is language. Where experiential background is limited and the ability to label is lacking, the school must provide learning experiences to make up the deficit. Early training in the basic intellectual skills is critical for future development.

Second, even children from privileged backgrounds need ever-increasing ability to symbolize as the learning tasks become more complex and concepts more abstract and sophisticated. Anyone at all familiar with college classes will verify the pitiable lack of ability to speak or to write cogently and coherently on the part of many students. The development of efficacy in language usage is a critical need in today's symbol-saturated world.

Human variability

Another area which has involved the thought and effort of some of the most scholarly minds in education is that of human variability. This concern is not new. Teachers have been talking about taking care of individual differences for a long time. But the "differences" which have been recognized are usually concerned with variation in academic achievement and the "taking care" has been directed at minimizing these differences so that all children can achieve at or above grade level.

4 Irving E. Sigel, "How Intelligence Tests Limit Understanding of Intelligence," in Ira J. Gordon (ed.), *Human Development* (Chicago: Scott, Foresman and Company, 1965), p. 289.

New insights concerning the "hard core" sources of variability and the plasticity of these sources provide a much more challenging and defensible goal. Education for tomorrow's complex world demands the nurturing of *individuality* and the task of the school *is to help each child become what he, and he alone, can be.* Acceptance of this goal raises some questions regarding the sources of human differentiation:

1. *Is the individual's I.Q. a fixed, immutable quality which sets the limits of his ability to learn?* Probably not! Evidence accumulates to substantiate the position that intelligence is highly modifiable and very sensitive to environmental factors. Writing in *Language Programs for the Disadvantaged,* Samuel A. Kirk says:

> The original, inherited potential of an individual, aside from environmental influences may not have been fixed but has a wide range of reaction to varying influences. Similarly, even the organism which results from genetic, prenatal, and paranatal influences probably has a reaction range within which variation may result from life experiences. Perhaps we should say that an individual has an I.Q.—not of 80 or 60 or 120—but of 80 to 120 or 120 to 160, and that how an individual develops after birth is dependent on the interaction with the environment. So this individual may have an I.Q. of 80 with a poor environment or 120 with a good environment. I think that is the kind of range within which we operate culturally, educationally and environmentally.[5]

Studies of children who have been removed from barren, restrictive environments to more favorable situations show a continuing increase of the children's measurable I.Q. that presumably resulted from the expansion and enrichment of their perceptual fields. In this connection Arthur W. Combs writes:

> This is, indeed, an interesting notion, for it means that the individual's capacity for intelligent behavior is dependent upon the state of his perceptual field. It means that human capacities are perhaps not as limited as we have been inclined to think. If human capacities for intelligent behavior are dependent on perception, then they are far more open to

    [5] Samuel A. Kirk, "Language, Intelligence and the Educability of the Disadvantaged," in *Language Programs for the Disadvantaged* (Washington, D.C.: National Council of Teachers of English, 1965), p. 250.

change than we have ever supposed. Indeed, human perceptions are so much within our capacity that we may even be able to create intelligence by helping people to perceive more extensively and more richly and by creating situations that make it possible for those perceptions to be available when needed.[6]

2. *Is intelligence a unilateral, one-dimensional capacity of generalized ability?* No, says recent research. There are probably many kinds of intelligence. On the basis of insights derived from factor analysis, J. P. Guilford and his associates have identified some 50 different primary mental abilities. This classification contrasts sharply with the 1 to 5 abilities measured by most intelligence tests and used by teachers as a basis for the instructional program. The need for the school to reorganize its program in the light of these varying abilities is pointed up by this statement by George W. Denemark:

> Education must recognize that the school population represents many kinds of ability and many levels of talent. . . . Our conception of excellence must embrace many kinds of achievement at many levels of performance. No single scale or simple set of categories will be adequate to measure excellence. There may be excellence in abstract intellectual activity, in art, in music, in managerial activity, in craftsmanship, in technical work, to mention but a few. Intelligence and excellence have many dimensions, many variations among children. All must be recognized. All must be planned for.[7]

3. *Are there certain dimensions of human productivity that may require the schools' special attention in matters of identification and development?* Certainly creative ability must be recognized in this category. One of the strangest incongruencies in contemporary American society is that the educational institution gives little but neglect or disapproval to the ability which nurtured its greatness and can enhance its further progress. Concern with creativity is not a new phenomenon on the education scene; writing and re-

6 Combs, *op cit.,* p. 13.
7 George W. Denemark, "Human Variability and Learning: Implications for Education," in Walter B. Waetjin (ed.), *Human Variability and Learning* (Washington, D.C.: Association for Supervision and Curriculum Development, 1961), p. 7.

search in the field date back at least to the turn of the century. It is included here because of the lack of implementation for its development and because more recent research emphasizes its critical importance.

Again, we give lip service to the desirability of divergence but we behave as though we value convergency, conformity, and verbalism. We *say* that we strive to give children opportunities to inquire, to explore, and to make choices; we *teach* them only *what to think* and how to reproduce it in testing situation.

One factor which explains this inconsistency is our continued reliance on traditional measures of intelligence. It has been estimated that performance on I.Q. tests will fail to identify 70 per cent of those who have the highest degree of creative ability. According to Guilford,

Creative aptitudes compose a segment of intelligence, but of a much broader conception of intelligence than is usually held. It is a badly neglected segment, for the creative abilities have been almost entirely overlooked in customary tests of intelligence. I.Q. tests by origin and by subsequent emphases have stressed a very few intellectual abilities that are obviously important for success in school, and success in school has been assessed in a way that emphasizes the same basic abilities. The "intelligence" of which most writers speak is actually more properly regarded as academic ability. Neither academic-aptitude tests nor academic-achievement measures have given any weight to creative performance except in very rare instances.[8]

Characteristics which seem to have the greatest validity in the identification of the creatively gifted include spontaneity, flexibility, originality, and fluency of expression, association, and vocabulary. These are also the characteristics of childhood! Creativity is not a gift restricted to a favored few. All children possess it to some indeterminate degree. The challenge is obvious. The school must provide a rich variety of ideas, a fund of stimulating symbols, and a climate which accepts and values uniqueness.

[8] J. P. Guilford, "A Psychometric Approach to Creativity," in Harold H. Anderson (ed.), *Creativity in Childhood and Adolescence* (Palo Alto, Calif.: Science and Behavior Books, 1965), p. 8.

4. *Does the suggested scope of human variability have other significant implications for educational thought and practice?* This must be answered with an emphatic "Yes." The first implication is what might be called categorical thinking. We classify children into chronological age groups as though age were the sole factor in determining readiness for learning. But varying abilities from radically different experiential backgrounds deny the validity of this position. Then we categorize the age groups into grade groups even though all capable teachers know that they do not, and cannot, teach one "grade." And, finally, we bundle up the results of man's accumulated knowledge into neat little learning packages with complete disregard for the child's personal needs and the limits set by his perceptual field. John I. Goodlad writes to this point:

> Analyses of achievement test data generally collected by teachers reveal a startling range of pupil accomplishments. In the usual fourth grade class, for example:
> • The range in over-all average achievement is about four years, or about the same number as the grade-level designation. The range in reading is from six to eight years.
> • Only 10 to 15 percent of the class (not 50 percent, as most commonly estimated by teachers) are at grade level in all subjects by midyear.
> • Among the larger percentage of children presenting irregular patterns of achievement, there are some who vary from subject to subject by as much as four years.[9]

Organizational patterns and instructional practices must be revised to accommodate such individuality. In most cases, the most practical start is for each teacher to extinguish his grade-mindedness and provide learning tasks which are appropriate to the established needs of the learners and adjustable in terms of difficulty and complexity to their developmental levels.

Preoccupation with arbitrary age-grade standards has another implication. This has to do with the effects of threat. When a child is unable to accomplish prescribed work, he is threatened—with

9 John I. Goodlad, "What About Nongrading Our Schools?" in Maurie Hillson (ed), *Changes and Innovation in Elementary School Organization* (New York: Holt, Rinehart and Winston, Inc., 1965), pp. 378–379.

rejection, retention, or punishment. His perceptions focus or "close in" on the threatening situation; he becomes anxious, hostile, and defensive. No desirable learning can occur in this circumstance, for the child is too busy defending his own integrity.

It seems certain that much of the failure and many of the stress situations in the elementary school are caused by language-related deficiencies. So the final implication derived from what we know about learning and what we know about the learner provides the basis for the remaining chapters of this book. Children need language experiences which are perceived as being related to their own purposes, which allow individuality and diversity, which stimulate personal involvement and challenge real thought, and which provide for continuity of progress. Since oral language provides the basis for the development of other language skills and facilitates learning, many of these experiences must involve oral communication. The techniques and procedures suggested in succeeding chapters were designed to meet these criteria.

three
The stock in trade
words, words, words!

On an automobile trip to a rather distant city a three-year-old was told that the family would stop for dinner at a place where a light could be seen atop a tall tower. The eager little fellow looked and looked for the light and, finally, greatly exasperated by the enforced waiting, said, "I can't see any light 'twinkin.' " This same child, at home, wanted to play under the lawn sprinkler. He came to his mother with his request. "Make it 'sprink,' " he demanded.

Young children who have had a wide background of experience and much exposure to books and to adult verbalization use beautifully descriptive language. Theirs is the most comfortable, most rhythmical, and most interesting language to be heard. If they don't know a word to use, they coin one. The three- and four-year-olds enjoy experimenting with words, especially the polysyllabic words that roll off their tongues like the mountain brooks roll among the rocks. One was fascinated with *exceptional.* For several days his reaction to every statement that he heard was "That's 'ceptional,' " followed by a pleased giggle. Another one discovered *delicious,* and everything he tasted, or wanted to taste, was "very 'licious." They use effective language to convey new concepts and feelings, too. When one little boy realized that his father was as significant in his life as his beloved "Mommy" he revealed this feeling by saying *"My* Daddy"—never just "Daddy," always *"My* Daddy."

23

Whatever happens along the way to change the rich, vivid language of the young child to the sterile, monosyllabic language which characterizes so much of the oral expression of later years? Words are our stock in trade—the building blocks of oral communication.

Sensitivity to words

Mauree Applegate, one of the great masters of using the right word at the right time, tells us:

> No more useful legacy could a school teacher leave with her school children than to give them a feeling for words—an "insatiable curiosity" about words. Words can be tasted, smelled, heard, felt, seen, and put into action. They help us to understand the world we live in and the people we live with. They help us to know the false. *They help us to say exactly what we mean.* In diplomacy, if we do not have the right words, even our nation is in peril. The wrong word causes us to lose out in business and in the business of living. How many people know half as much about the right word to use as they know about the right costume to wear? [1]

The answer to Dr. Applegate's question is obvious—not many! This poses another question. What is done in the classrooms of the nation to develop sensitivity to words and vividness of expression? Again, not much! Few learning tasks are undertaken with the specific objective of expanding and enriching the learner's vocabulary, and these few are woefully ineffective. This writer has seen in use, and has been the victim of, the weekly "vocabulary list," a compilation of long words characterized chiefly by infrequency of use. Pupils are expected to "look up" such words as *chagrined, verbosity,* and *titillate* in their dictionaries, mark the accents and letter sounds, *write* the definitions, and *write* sentences containing the words. Is that vocabulary development?

As might be expected, the attitudes and skill of the teacher

---

[1] Mauree Applegate, *Helping Children Write* (Evanston, Ill.: Row, Peterson and Company, 1961), p. 131.

are the significant factors in the development of sensitivity to words. Many teachers, by reason of training and interest, are steeped in the tradition of reading good literature. They like to read, and they enjoy beautiful language. Others are not so fortunate. Years of association with young children and continued efforts to "talk on the child's level" make for sterile, unimaginative word usage. Teachers should not be so concerned with such rigid control of vocabulary. Children love new words, especially the big ones. They should occasionally have to rise to the necessity of gathering word meaning from context. Teachers will be surprised at their adroitness in doing this.

To the teacher who wants to work with children in developing a feeling for words, the restrictions of her own limited vocabulary need not be an obstacle. She can work along with them, and each new, colorful word will add richness to her language and to theirs. Each line of poetic prose or precise explanation will be a challenge to further progress. And each stimulating language experience will provide its own reinforcement.

The atmosphere in the classroom must be conducive to free expression and relaxed effort. The time schedule must be flexible, but aimless meandering is useless. Definite lesson plans aimed at specific objectives underlie each experience in vocabulary development. The enthusiasm of the teacher is contagious. The approval and appreciation expressed by the teacher are the catalytic agents to keep the broth brewing. Ample opportunities to use the new learnings in meaningful language situations are the final ingredient in a successful program.

The sensory words

There are many kinds of words. Probably those used to describe sensory reactions provide the best starting point in the word-building program. Here are some suggestions for the development of words related to seeing, hearing, feeling, smelling, and tasting.

1. Have a collection of items, such as a piece of fur, a square of sandpaper, a rock, and some damp spaghetti. Ask, "How does each one feel?" List the descriptive adjectives in columns on the

blackboard. If you are a primary teacher you may want to transfer
them to chart paper for future review. Try to get unusual responses
—slimy, rasping, silky, etc. Be sure to recognize these contributions
and be ready with suggestions of your own.

2. Divide the class into several small groups. Give each group
a "secret" object to taste—a lemon, an apple, a licorice stick, or a
banana. Have the members of the group compile a list of five or
six descriptive words to present to the class as a riddle. These words
may be listed on the board for purposes of visual discrimination.
Notice that the actual objects are suggested for use. The *experience*
of tasting stimulates a variety of responses. Pictures may be substituted later, after the children have had wide exposure to concrete
items.

3. "Heads down, eyes closed. No peeking!" The teacher makes
sounds—crumpling paper, humming a tune, slamming a door, or
opening and closing books. The children identify the sounds, one
by one, and think of words to describe them. Children may be
asked to think of more sound activities so that they may act as
leaders the following day.

4. Say, "Do you like to smell bacon frying when you get up
in the morning? I think it's my favorite smell. Who can think how
it smells? . . . *Delicious!* That's a very good word! *Appetizing?*
Of course! Who wants to give us a sentence about his favorite
smell?" The one who thinks of an exciting descriptive word may
then propose his favorite smell. The teacher may have a list of
"favorite smell" sentences to help children get started.

5. Phrase tag: The leader says, "Mary, on my way to school
this morning, I saw a miserable, frightened puppy." Mary must then
say, "Jennie, on my way to school this morning, I saw a sprightly,
saucy robin." Jennie continues the game, calling on another pupil.
Each one repeats the opening phrase and adds an object and two
modifiers. Young children may be asked for only one, sixth graders
for as many as three. Many other sentence beginnings may be used:

    a. When I went to the zoo, I saw _____.
    b. When we went to Washington, D.C., we saw _____.
    c. On our way to California, we saw _____.
    d. While we were visiting the fire station, I saw _____.

The emotionally charged words

The ability to recognize and use those words which have become emotionally charged through culturally determined connotations has a twofold significance. First, these words pertain to our deepest emotions and add vigor and sincerity to our speech. Second, people need to recognize that they are "used" by such words. These words are the prime factors in the sales pitch of the propagandist. Our extreme reactions to them can cause us to buy unwanted, shoddy merchandise, to accept prejudice as fact, to vote for ill-qualified, unscrupulous candidates, and, in extreme cases, to abandon the standards and principles we live by.

We can help children speak frankly and beautifully about their deepest emotions; that, of course, is exactly what the outstanding writers and speakers do. And we can make them aware of the pitfalls created by the words of those who prey on the emotions of mankind for their own selfish interests. The suggestions that follow may help accomplish these aims.

1. Analyze editorials from the local newspaper. Identify and discuss the words that make a sharp impact. Substitute mundane, everyday words for them to determine the full effect of word choice.

2. Listen to or read the wartime speeches of Franklin Roosevelt, Winston Churchill, and, in the upper grades, Hitler. Pick out a sampling of the "impact" words and discuss why they were used in their particular context.

3. Play a tape recording of a television commercial. What are the "sell" words and phrases? Let children make substitutions, working toward choices which are as effective as the original.

4. Develop a class scrapbook of especially striking advertisements. Discuss and identify the emotion to which each one appeals. List the words used on the board or under each picture. Add words to those used by the advertisers.

5. Develop a list of "leads" based on words which are emotionally charged. Examples of such leads are:

a. My *friend* is _____.
b. I *love* my grandmother because she is _____.

c. *Winning* a game makes me feel _____.
d. *Losing* a game makes one feel _____.
e. *Communism* is a form of government which is _____.
f. I prefer a *democratic* form of government because it is _____.

g. The words which best describe my *father* are _____.

Words relating to natural phenomena

The natural world offers a constant source of materials for vocabulary enrichment. Working with these materials supplies an abundance of concomitant learnings. The child develops an awareness of his surroundings, an appreciation of the orderliness of nature, and the habit of close observation. The concepts of space, time, and change, so difficult for the young learner to grasp, are strengthened and expanded for him. This source is such an easy one for the teacher, too. Seasons change, sunrise follows darkness, winds blow, waves crash, and snow flurries, all without the teacher's efforts of skimming, clipping, gathering, begging, borrowing, or searching. And natural phenomena are so precise, so prolific, and so puzzling that motivation is inherent. Teachers may want to try these ideas:

1. "Do you feel any different when the sun is shining from the way you do when the world is cloudy and dusky? Let's think of some words which tell how each kind of weather makes us feel." Seek to elicit the big, powerful words: *morose, exhilarated, energetic, gloomy.*

2. Word hunt: Keep a record of the weather each day for a week—sunny and mild, rainy and warm, cold and windy, mild and cloudy, gray and overcast. Divide the class into five groups. Which group can make the best list of words to describe its day?

3. Give children one or two minutes to think through their responses to "The most beautiful sight in the world is _____." Then each one gets one minute to give his report using his very best words to draw a mental picture of his choice.

4. Use "the sounds of nature" as the theme of a similar lesson. The teacher should give examples:

    a. How a cricket chirps.
    b. How a bobwhite calls.
    c. The sounds of a hurricane.
    d. The day of the blizzard.
    e. A rainstorm on a metal roof.
    f. The sounds of the sea.

5. Anecdotes about weather situations: Ask, "Did you ever have a birthday party in the snow, a picnic in the rain, a fishing trip in a storm? Can you think of words which accurately describe the situation or how you felt? Was it *hilarious, exciting, frightening,* or *depressing?*"

Words about people

People! Now here is the richest source of all! We live with them, love them, and hate them. We play with them, laugh with them, and work with them. People complicate and enrich our lives and change the course of history. We wonder about them, worry about them, and think about them. The complexity and diversity of human behavior and personality are an ever-present challenge to one who would describe them. If we would have children cognizant of the need for language power, we would do well to exploit this field of vocabulary expansion. Teachers may like to try some of these suggestions:

1. My-favorite-person game: The first person says, "My favorite person is kind"; the second says, "My favorite person is kind and gentle"; the third says, "My favorite person is kind, gentle, and honest." Each participant adds another descriptive word at the end of the list. Listening skills are highly involved here, as they are in most techniques for vocabulary development.

2. Storybook friends: Each pupil can identify his favorite book characters: Tom Sawyer, Curious George, Caddie Woodlawn, Henry Huggins, Karana. Descriptive words may be used as riddles for classmates to guess the character, or the child may tell the group about his choice.

3. Listen-carefully game: Children may hear tape recordings of voices—the principal's, the teacher's, a former teacher's, the Presi-

dent's, a well-known senator's, those of members of the class. Then talk about them. Are they *high, low, gruff, rasping, loud, soft, angry,* or *pleasing?*

4. The movements of people provide an interesting source of contrast. Pupils may pantomime a *sloucher,* a *shuffler,* a *runner,* or an *ambler.* Then use the sitting position in a similar way. People don't just sit—they *sprawl, lounge,* or *slump.*

5. People aren't just short or tall, fat or slim, big or little, either. Use the fat man in the circus or a famous football lineman to introduce such words as *obese, immense, huge,* and *gigantic.* Use a "Barbie" doll, a well-known basketball player, or a midget to develop lists of words pertaining to size.

6. Don't forget the mood and personality-trait words. How do you describe the *talker,* the *glowerer,* the *sparkler,* the *weeper?* Make a list of all the personality images you can think of.

Other word clusters

This big world is so "full of a number of things" that there is an infinite supply to be discussed, labeled, and described. Many of the suggestions listed previously can be adapted to the development of vocabularies pertaining to:

1. Sounds, sights, smells, and movement of the big city. Young children may think of *busy, noisy,* and *crowded,* but wouldn't alert sixth graders have a field day with *cacophony, odoriferous, raucous,* and *teeming?*

2. Farm and country life. The quiet words to describe the countryside provide an interesting contrast to the city words. Let children respond to *serene, serenity, pastoral, murmuring, meandering,* and *lowing.*

3. Transportation and space exploration. This aspect of modern life is a major interest of boys and girls. Teachers would do well to exploit this interest. All of the words having to do with rapid movement and powerful action can be used in discussions and word games centered on these subjects.

4. Recreation and sports. Here, too, is another area of interest to young people. Words pertaining to pleasure and fun,

words describing the attributes of sportsmanship, words of action —all of these, and many more, apply to this subject.

5. Food, clothing, and shelter. These are necessities of living and are, of course, areas of concern to everyone. The social studies in the elementary school are frequently centered on these topics, and vocabulary development can be correlated with these subjects.

The list of opportunities could continue on and on. Alert, imaginative teachers will never be at a loss for new and stimulating ideas for vocabulary development. Nor will such teachers ever permit the program to degenerate into meaningless vocabulary drills or subjects for Friday's test. If we really want children to be sensitive to words, we will provide them with situations in which words are talked about, heard, treasured, and *used*.

Preciseness and specificity in language usage

Thus far this chapter has emphasized the need for the elementary schools to become consciously and actively involved in programs aimed at vocabulary expansion and enrichment. The child's ability to speak well and, consequently, his ability to write and read well depend largely on the number and quality of the words he can use. There is, however, another prerequisite to effective oral communication. This is, of course, the exactness of his word choice. A recent publication by Walter T. Petty and Mary E. Bowen contains this statement:

> One of the skills in working with words is knowing the very best and most exact way of getting across ideas. Well-equipped writers don't have to grope for a word; they choose one. Some study of synonyms comes up with routine class work, but much more can be done.[2]

It is quite true that much more can be done. And it can be done in ways that facilitate real learning and pleasure in speaking. A sensitive, creative student teacher was working with a group of

[2] Walter T. Petty and Mary E. Bowen, *Slithery Snakes and Other Aids to Children's Writing* (New York: Appleton-Century-Crofts, 1967), p. 41.

third graders. The group had just finished reading an animal story, and one little boy made the comment that the horse surely could run fast. "Yes," replied the teacher, "He could run very fast, but another word was used in place of *run* in the story. Can anyone remember what it was? . . . Yes, it was *gallop*. Do you think galloping is different from running? Perhaps we can act it out." ("Acting it out" was a favorite technique in that class.)

One child showed what *galloping* means; another demonstrated *running*. Then the teacher suggested that horses use other gaits. The children identified *walking, trotting,* and *cantering.* The teacher told the group that most animals can run but that many animals have distinctive movements that can be described more accurately by using words other than *run.* She dismissed the group with this assignment: "Go to your seats. Each one put on his thinking cap and choose an animal which runs in a particular manner. Tomorrow, each of you may 'act out' the way your animal runs. The rest of us will try to guess what animal you are imitating and what word best describes it."

The college supervisor (this writer) could hardly wait until the next day. After rearranging the entire observation schedule, she arrived in this third-grade classroom to see a kangaroo *leaping,* an elephant *lumbering,* a panther *slinking,* a rabbit *hopping* (one girl said hippity-hopping), a lion *stalking,* and a snake *slippering* ("I don't think that is a word; perhaps you mean *slithering,*" said the teacher).

It was one of the most stimulating lessons I have ever witnessed. The children were interested and excited, but, more important, the learning task was accomplishing the goal which Richard Corbin discusses when he says:

A large vocabulary may be one indication of a person's intelligence level, but it is no guarantee that he will be effective as a writer. English is blessed with one of the largest supplies of synonyms of any language in the world. Was last evening's much publicized television spectacle *abominable, corrupting, depraved, evil, immoral, pernicious, vicious, unwholesome, worthless*—or merely *bad?* The fact that one child described it as having been *pernicious* may be impressive, but it may also be inaccurate. The ability to choose the *exact* rather than the "big" word is one sign of a good writer and a sound thinker.[3]

[3] Richard Corbin, *The Teaching of Writing in Our Schools* (New York: The Macmillan Company, 1966), p. 69.

The following suggestions may be helpful to the teacher who recognizes the importance of using the *specific* word at the right time and place.

1. Have each child keep his own word book. It may be started with a picture of a landscape. Is the mountain *tall?*; is it *high?*; is it *towering?* Write an exact descriptive word under the picture. Putting the word in a sentence to be used as the caption will serve to develop "sentence sense," too. After the class has decided on several exact words, let each child choose his own and tell the group about his choice. As time permits, add more pictures, and then clippings and poems in which specificity of word choice may be noted or substituted.

2. Substitute exact words for the vague, mundane generalizations used in most conversation and writing. The pupil may say, "These flowers were growing everywhere." Mark off columns on the blackboard in this manner:

What kinds of flowers?	How were they growing?	Where were they growing?
The wildflowers	were growing profusely	everywhere I looked.
These blue larkspur	completely covered	every field and meadow.
Every conceivable kind of wildflower	decorated	the rolling hillside.

As the children grow in skill and imagination, increase the complexity of the columns to include the specific study of adjectives, adverbs, similes, and metaphors.

Other suggested generalizations:

   a. The rain was falling.
   b. My birthday was fun.
   c. We played in the snow.
   d. That boy is my friend.
   e. April is a nice month.
   f. Our baby is cute.
   g. The moon is full.

3. Synonym baseball: Divide the class into teams. Prepare a list of common words which have multiple synonyms. If a pupil can name one, he goes to first base; another one named by a team-

mate advances the runner to second. The naming of two synonyms will achieve a double; four, of course, is a home run.

As children become more word conscious and more interested in vocabulary expansion, the teacher will need to point out the difference between the *denotation* of a word and the *connotation*. *Denotation* refers to the dictionary meaning of the word; *connotation* refers to the implications obtained through popular usage. Certain words which may be listed as synonyms are not synonymous in connotation. Corbin speaks to this point when he writes:

> The synonyms *slender* and *skinny* show the denotation "thin, not fat." The connotation of the former is "attractively or becomingly thin," whereas the latter suggests "unpleasant boniness." In one or another, most of the important words that we use carry an extra meaning. Not to be aware of this is to miss a good deal of what is said and written, for the full meaning of a word consists of both its denotation and its connotation.[4]

Efforts to improve oral communication through vocabulary enrichment should not break down into a petty hassle over minute semantic differences in words, but at least some elementary pupils would profit from noticing that *pretty* and *beautiful* are used to connote entirely different kinds of feminine appearances, and a *small* person is not necessarily *petite*. Children should at least be aware of this facet of word usage.

Words—the symbols we attach to objects, feelings, and appearances, the vehicles of human thought and communication—are important. The elementary school affects every aspect of the child's development; planned, conscientious efforts to provide him with colorful building blocks of communication will help him become an effective participant in his social world and a fully functioning, self-actualizing individual.

4 *Ibid.*

four
Creative dramatics
play like i'm a mommy

Two 3½-year-olds were playing back of a large reclining chair in the corner of the den. Mark said, "Be careful, Lawrency [Lawrence]. There's a monster in there."

Lawrence looked a little startled, but, like any imaginative little boy, he rallied his creative forces and replied, "A green monster—with big ears; he'll get us."

"He *eats* people! Let's knock on the door and scare him." Mark was literally jumping with excitement.

"All right! Be ready to run. There's some little monsters, too. They're too little. They can't catch us." Lawrence was getting braver as he rationalized his fear.

Mark was glad to accept this. He knocked on the wall, exclaiming, "Hey, monsters! You can't get me. I can run fast."

Both little boys raced to the middle of the room and fell on the floor laughing, delighted with themselves and their game.

Kim and Annette, two four-year-old girls, played a different game as their mothers played bridge.

Said Annette, "Play like I'm a mommy and you're a mommy."

"Okay," agreed Kim, "you be at your house and I'll be at mine, and I'll call you on the telephone."

She picked up the imaginary receiver and dialed the number. Annette answered. "Hello," she said, "I'm Mommy, and I'm so mad!

35

The darn washin' 'chine is broked. Can you send your daddy over to fix it?"

"No, he can't come." Kim was very positive about this. "He said he ain't at home. He's taking a nap."

"Oh—well, good-bye," said Annette, and the game ended.

One doesn't have to eavesdrop long on the conversation of young children to realize that dramatic play is a favorite vehicle for self-expression. Sometimes their topic is an imaginary situation related to something they've seen or heard. The "monsters" theme of the first anecdote undoubtedly came from television. More frequently, the dramatic play of the preschooler is aimed at the need for role identification. Kim and Annette were learning to be future "mommies." So are all the millions of little girls who teeter around in mothers' high heels, swinging purses as large as they are, and, for better or for worse, mimicking the adult females they know.

A definition

Drama is an art form, and, as such, it is vigorously structured and highly developed. What, then, do we mean by dramatic play and creative dramatics for children, and how do they fit into the elementary-school curriculum? For our purposes, "creative dramatics" refers to the creation by children of situations, scenes, or plays requiring improvised speech. The guidance of a sensitive teacher is a necessary ingredient, and the personal development of the learners rather than audience appeal is the goal.

In more technical and more comprehensive discussions of the area, there is a further delineation between creative play and creative dramatics. Creative play is thought of as the natural expression of children with no set dramatic form. It may concern riding in a train, playing in a mud puddle, or crossing the street at a busy corner. It has no defined beginning or ending. Creative dramatics, on the other hand, has a well-defined dramatic form involving a beginning, a strong story element, a climax, and a conclusion. Usually, creative play is used with small children, and creative dramatics is used in the intermediate and upper grades. Since the emphasis here is on techniques for the development of oral language and since few children have had wide exposure to these experiences, the two terms are used almost interchangeably but with a strong orientation toward the elements of creative play.

The values of creative play

All techniques and procedures used in the classroom must be educationally defensible. Each specific learning task should contribute to the development of the learner and should be planned and implemented with well-defined behavioral objectives. The educational values of creative dramatics are multiple. The use of dramatic play is not "gimmick teaching" designed to keep children entertained. Winifred Ward writes:

> A classroom teacher need never apologize for using a dramatic approach in her teaching. She may not see its effect at first because of her lack of experience in using it skillfully. If she is sincere in trying it, however, she will be surprised at the enthusiastic way in which her children will respond. For she will be appealing to a universal interest, and both she and her children will learn more than is written in their books.[1]

A value frequently cited for creative play is the inherent opportunity it affords for the release of emotional tension. Its therapeutic value is basic to the procedures of play therapy, which is widely used in the treatment of troubled children. So, too, as children act out the play situations in the classroom, their deepest preoccupations and concerns are revealed. That enables the teacher to provide guidance and help where possible. The actual verbalization of the problem may be beneficial to the child, too, because it serves to define and limit the situation and, thereby, to bring it to manageable terms.

A fifth-grade group was giving a play about the westward movement in the United States. The scene involved choosing a person to act as the scout for the wagon train, and the players were discussing the qualities needed in the person on this position. One

[1] Winifred Ward, *Playmaking with Children,* second edition (New York: Appleton-Century-Crofts, 1957), p. 272.

rather heavy boy said, "I am *so* brave enough. Maybe I can't do some of the tricks others can, but I'm brave and strong." The teacher, who had noticed this child's reluctance to participate in playground activities, talked to the principal about his improvised comment. Together, they persuaded his mother to diminish his calorie intake, and they asked the playground director to give him extra help with batting and throwing skills. This was a long-term solution, but the results were gratifying. Creative dramatics had pinpointed the problem.

The need for the development of satisfactory personal relationships and the need for social cooperation are critical to a world of technological automation and urban anonymity. The contributions of creative play to the fulfillment of these needs is aptly described by Geraldine Siks:

> Creative dramatics by its very nature is a group art. It calls for teamwork. It requires cooperation in planning, playing and evaluating. It provides a play situation where children experience basic rules for living with others. They learn to take turns, respect one another, avoid interruptions. Each child is given opportunities to be both a leader and a member of a group working together in some form of concerted effort for the success of a scene or experience. A child constantly yields to discipline as he joins with others to create and express.[2]

This statement points up another value of creative dramatics, the opportunity provided for the structuring of values and attitudes. As children interact in the freedom of these play situations they develop sensitivity to human needs and emotions and empathy with the feelings and beliefs of others. They learn to value individuality and to respect variability.

Teachers are understandably concerned about the development of listening skills. The effects of not listening are too apparent to be ignored. Every teacher is far too familiar with the "I don't know what you said to do" syndrome. We are told that almost 60 percent of the child's school day is spent listening. This is indeed unfortunate. Children need to be more actively involved in the learning process than such figures indicate them to be, but the

---

[2] Geraldine Brain Siks, *Creative Dramatics* (New York: Harper & Row, Publishers, 1958), pp. 27–28.

fact remains that there is growing emphasis on the need for techniques to develop effective listening habits. Creative dramatics offers a golden opportunity in this area. Listening is involved in every step of the process. Creative play provides an excellent medium for learning:

1. willingness to listen attentively,
2. the ability to identify the main point,
3. the ability to listen for the sequence of events,
4. the ability to listen for subordinate ideas and substantiating data,
5. the ability to listen for precise and vivid words and sentences,
6. the ability to listen for interesting aspects of a story.

Creative play has other, concomitant educational values. It helps children to identify main ideas and to organize their thoughts. It encourages creative thinking because it requires sensitivity, originality, flexibility, and the abilities to analyze, synthesize, and redefine, and it promotes problem solving as children cope with the complexities of the situational demands.

For the immediate purposes of this book, the main point is that creative dramatics requires oral expression in a functional, interesting situation. The particular speech patterns, sentence structure, and word choice in a dramatic situation reveal a great deal about the child's language development and his language needs. The demands of the situation foster constantly expanding language facility requiring the child to be aware of:

1. precision of language,
2. vividness of language,
3. effects of regional and cultural influences on language,
4. multiple word meanings,
5. melody and rhythm in language,
6. the various functions of words in a sentence,
7. the need for continuity and coherence in language expression,
8. the need for acceptable enumeration, pleasing modulation, and correct pronunciation,
9. the effects of rate, pitch, and volume of speech.

The teacher and her responsibilities

After all the courses are taken, all the books read, all the manuals and curriculum guides studied, and all the conversations in the teachers' lounge noted, it is, in the final analysis, the teacher herself who determines the actual instructional program which is followed in the classroom. The most important question is, then, what kind of person with what kinds of special competences and unique personality traits will be a successful teacher of creative dramatics. The answer is relatively simple. Any teacher who really *wants* to make this technique a significant factor in the learning program can do so!

The most readily identifiable weakness in many programs of creative dramatics is the formalized structure of the presentations. It seems perfectly obvious to say that the teacher who would work effectively in this area must *like* children. An important clarification is necessary. She must like children who *act* and *sound* like children, not like little robots drilled to adult standards of perfection by endless rehearsals.

The successful teacher of dramatics is a master disciplinarian in the very best, and only acceptable, sense of that word. Her learners are as self-directed and self-controlled as their age level and previous experience will allow. The time that has been taken to help the children establish their own standards of conduct and to evaluate their progress, the individual conferences with children who have difficulty, and her firmness and consistency bring rich rewards. There is order without rigidity, freedom without chaos, and responsibility without frustration.

Creativity thrives on and reacts to beauty! The teacher who plans a creative instructional program must be attractive, well-groomed, and tastefully dressed. Every person can't be beautiful, but everyone can wear clear, vibrant colors in becoming styles, an interesting piece of jewelry, carefully applied makeup, and attractively styled hair. The day of the stereotyped dowdy, overdressed (in last year's Sunday best) "little old lady" schoolteacher is gone! This teacher's voice is pleasant, too, because she knows that her enunciation and articulation serve as models for her children and that a tense, high-pitched voice will destroy the relaxed, warm emotional climate that is a prerequisite to any creative endeavor.

Summing up, the teacher of creative dramatics must be a warm, sensitive individual who sees its implications for the development of oral communication skills, and who is willing to explore its possibilities. She knows children and respects their ability to be self-directing, autonomous little individuals. Finally, she herself is excited about learning and about new avenues to learning, and her enthusiasm kindles the fires of creativity in her children.

Setting the stage

It has long been recognized that the physical appearance and arrangement of the classroom can have a direct effect on learning, facilitating or impeding it. This is especially true in the area of creative play. A light, well-ventilated room is a necessity. Children can neither think well nor move well in a stuffy, overheated atmosphere. Space is very important, too. An informal room arrangement, with chairs or desks arranged around the periphery of a large open space, is best. There must be room to move about, and the observers should have a clear view of the action without having to peer around people or objects. Most modern classrooms are decorated in attractive colors. How wonderful! The muddy browns and beiges of yesterday may have saved money for maintenance departments, but they did little to stimulate creative thought.

Teachers would do well to think beyond the four walls of the classroom for their settings, too. Some of the best experiences in creative play may take place in the shade of the big tree in the corner of the school yard. Nature does a pretty good job of providing an attractive atmosphere. The gymnasium or auditorium offers a possibility, and porches are fine!

Children do not create in a vacuum, nor do they talk unless they have something to talk about. Many concrete and vicarious experiences provide the pegs on which they hang creative communication. Field trips around the school yard, to the zoo, to the fire station, and to the bakery give them insights into human activities and natural phenomena. The use of films, filmstrips, tape recordings, phonograph records, and transparencies broadens their horizons. Sharing books, hearing stories and poetry, seeing plays, and attending concerts develop awareness and sensitivity. Attractive bulletin boards, charts, science, and social studies materials and displays create interest and enthusiasm. A diversified instructional program and a rich classroom environment are necessary to the successful development of creative play activities.

The type of creative activities recommended here do not require, and, indeed, should not use, elaborate costumes or props. Children may occasionally make costumes of large brown paper bags or old sheets or crepe paper, and, sometimes, they may paint a backdrop or construct a simple prop. But emphasis on the mechanical aspects is sure to detract from the central objectives—the wholesome development of children and their language power.

There are, however, two kinds of simple props which may be used to great advantage. The first of these is hats! Put a discarded or an improvised hat on a child player and interesting things happen. An old slouch hat produces the disreputable-looking Huck Finn; a plumed chapeau creates a magnificent "grand dame"; a straw hat encourages an authentic farmer or a beachcomber. The mere addition of hats makes soldiers stand straighter and march better or a birthday party come to life. No well-equipped classroom can be without a box full of hats and a file of easy patterns for use in constructing hats.

The second useful aid is puppets. The pupils who have never been able to break through their shyness to make oral contributions can participate freely if they're "hiding behind" puppets. Simple hand puppets can be made from so many things that the procurement of materials is never a problem.

One delightful puppet play portrayed the battle between the "villain" foods and the "hero" foods for the interest of "Johnny," the would-be ball player. King Koke was a soft-drink bottle with a cork head and a crown; Butch Bubble Gum and Lila Lollipop were made with construction paper heads and paper-bag clothing; Princess Sweet-Milk's head was a small milk carton, and Conchita Banana's was a stuffed casing of yellow material marked with a felt pen.

Teachers and children have used old socks and paper sacks with faces painted or crayoned. Puppet heads may be made of papier-mâché, corks, styrofoam balls, or small rubber balls; clothes are fashioned of scraps of dress material, crepe paper, or paper sacks; facial features and hair may be made with bits of yarn or embroidery thread, buttons, beads, paints, or stitches. Keep a box of supplies on hand and let the children make their own puppets. The experience provides a wonderful art lesson and allows the children time to identify with the characters they'll be portraying.

Planning the lesson

Planning for the session in creative play is as important, and follows the same pattern, as planning for any other lesson. The following guide is an excellent, concise outline of any easy-to-follow procedure. It is quoted from a paper prepared by Mrs. Dorothy Schwartz:

Plan, Play, Evaluate [3]

1. Plan

a. Teacher motivates children's thinking along lines of material she is going to use (i.e., plays a record, shows a foreign coin).

b. Presents material—tells or reads a story or poem, or shares an idea from which to create.

c. Guides the children to planning of the dramatization; helps them to focus their thinking and organize their ideas.

2. Play

a. May begin with group pantomimes (i.e., an activity pantomime such as eating fruit, or simultaneous characterizations).

b. Should select cast for playing according to needs of children. Combine in cast shy children and extroverts. There should be one child in the cast who can keep play moving. Every child in group should have opportunity to play. Stress importance of an OBSERVING AUDIENCE.

c. Start and stop playing with dramatic effect—"Places! In character! Curtain!" and "Cut!"

3. Evaluate

a. Teacher should set a constructive tone in evaluation. "What did

[3] From "Creative Dramatics," an unpublished mimeographed manuscript by Mrs. Dorothy T. Schwartz, Speech-Drama Consultant, State Department of Education, Montgomery, Alabama. Reprinted by permission.

you like about the playing?" "How could we make it more interesting next time?"

   b. Use indirect but leading questions to get children to make suggestions for improvement. Give each child's suggestion consideration.

   c. Encouragement is the keynote in effective evaluation. In offering suggestions, use the name of the character, rather than the name of the child who played the role.

   d. Concentrate on essentials—select two or more of the following for emphasis at a session:

(1) Teamwork	(5) Grouping
(2) Characterization	(6) Dialogue
(3) Pantomime	(7) Tempo (Timing)
(4) Story (Points in the scene)	(8) Climax

(9) Voice and Diction (Not too soon)

   e. Sum up two or three important suggestions for children before choosing next cast.

The developmental program

   Probably the best place to start the program in creative dramatics is with the simplest type of pantomime. Traditionally, pantomime was as highly structured and symbolic as the ballet. Certain gestures symbolized certain ideas, and style, rather than feeling, was the goal of the actor. Pantomime with children is not symbolic; it is as free and natural as the young child himself. It is, indeed, the language of childhood, for the child imitates what he sees others do. So, we begin with activity pantomimes.

   Say to the children, "It was raining so hard when I came to school this morning, I had to wear rain shoes and carry an umbrella. The wind was blowing, too. Who can show how I walked to school? Don't say a word! Just *show* us how you think I walked this morning."

   It is better to choose several children for the initial efforts. They will be more spontaneous in a group. Make encouraging comments as they move about: "Good, Janey! I *did* jump over a mud puddle!" "Look at Tom! He acts as if I *enjoyed* walking in the rain." "What do you suppose Susan is doing? She's *pulling* at something."

   Then talk about the pantomime. Ask them what else you

might have done (jumped across the gutter, turned the umbrella wrong-side out, or dropped a book in the puddle). How can you show that the wind was blowing or when the rain stopped? Let other children (as many as *want* to) try to do the same thing. Work on it till the children see some *improvement,* but be sure to stop before their interest lags.

There are literally hundreds of ideas for activity pantomimes. Try some of these:

1. Finding ants in the picnic food.
2. Looking for seashells.
3. Walking in cold water.
4. Helping mother wash the dishes.
5. Making cookies.

Then move on to pantomiming characters from books and poetry for children. Do "Poor Tired Tim," "Little Miss Muffet," "Choosing Shoes," and "Hickory Dickory Dock" or, for older children, "The Merry-Go-Round," "Homer Price," and "Mafatu." And, finally, work on sensory perception. Show how you look when you try to eat a lemon, a big juicy apple, and a banana. Pantomime hearing strange noises during the night or smelling the delicious odors of Christmas cookies.

The next step involves the use of dramatic play. The natural beginning point is with a situation they all know: "Let's act out our trip on the train! What did we do first? How many special characters do we need? Who wants to be the ticket agent? The conductor? Are we ready? All right—Places! In character! Curtain!"

Teachers will think of many situations to use dramatic play. Classroom standards may be acted out as children show "how we go to the lunchroom" or "how we get ready to go home." New playground games may be dramatized so that rules and procedures are clearly understood. Groups may "play" a taffy pull, a pillow fight, or a birthday party. Dramatic play is similar to pantomime in that it involves no dialogue and depends upon facial expression and body movement to convey meaning. It differs from pantomime in that the action is more sustained and a sequence of ideas is utilized.

Dialogue is introduced into the dramatic play situation as the story element becomes stronger and as children see the need for words to express the action. The teacher will recognize that a dramatic situation requiring dialogue and sustained action is a much more complex activity than the pantomime. Approach it with care, building the new skills and understandings with enthusiasm and patience. Help the children see that the use of speech follows a three-step pattern: we receive a stimulus of some sort (seeing, feeling, or hearing something), we think about it, and we talk about it. Demonstrate this with the use of a short phrase such as "Oh, look at that!" Say to the children, "I'm walking along the seashore and seeing all kinds of interesting things." Walk along, stopping to examine imaginary objects or to pick up seashells, then stop suddenly, point to something, and exclaim, "Oh! Look at that!" Let the children follow the sequence of speech use (see, think, and speak) and guess what you saw. Then put some of them in a similar situation. With younger children, the teacher may set the stage; older children can do their own. The players say the phrase when they "see" a beautiful birthday cake, a dog chasing a cat, the clutter when the box of crayons is spilled, etc. Comment on how the tone and pitch of the voice can show amazement, disgust, or excitement. Use more phrases to dramatize stimuli of other sensory perceptions.

The initial work with sustained dialogue should be done with small groups. The children will need guidance in "thinking through" the episode and in choosing dialogue to carry the action. If the group is planning a trip to the shopping center, the specific characters must be identified and defined. Shall we have Mother and Daddy and their two children or Grandmother and Auntie and two children? Do the children want to go to different stores or to buy different things? Are they well-behaved youngsters or spoiled brats? If Daddy had to take one of them back to the car what would he say? What would Grandmother say if she left her purse at the toy center? What kind of person is Grandmother? Old? Kind? Cranky? Generous? Remember that Grandmother must speak a certain way, walk a certain way, talk a certain way! The one who plays the part of Grandmother must *be* Grandmother throughout the episode.

This is a good time to work on speech problems that have been identified. Many of the difficulties with pronunciation of the difficult initial consonants can be eliminated by short periods of concentration on the time-honored "Peter Piper picked . . ." or

"She sells seashells. . . ." Long lists of tongue twisters are available in anthologies. Children enjoy writing their own, too.

Some of the less articulate children may be disturbed by these new demands, so it is important to use familiar group situations. Some of these situations might be:

1. A family shopping trip to the bakery or supermarket.
2. A child and his mother choosing a toy at the toy counter.
3. A group of Halloween trick-or-treaters.
4. Brothers and sisters choosing a Christmas gift for mother.
5. A family visit to the fair.
6. The family eating Thanksgiving dinner.
7. Susan's birthday party.
8. Introducing Mother to the teacher and the principal.
9. Telephone conversations to plan a party.
10. The group's ride on the train or trip to the airport.

The final step in the developmental program is story dramatization. This combines all the elements of the other phases and adds a strong story interest and a definite structure. A story has a beginning, which introduces the characters, gives the locale, and sets the mood; a climax, which brings an end to the conflict; and a conclusion, which summarizes the results of the action. The teacher must make sure that the learners can identify these elements. After she tells or reads the story, she helps the children analyze it for their presentation. They must know:

1. Where the story takes place. How will this information be conveyed to the audience?
2. What happens in the story. What is the first significant episode? The second? Which one is most important? How will we end our play?
3. Who the characters are. How do they look and talk and move? Do we want to "try on" these characters to see which ones each of you may fit?

Begin with short, simple stories with few episodes and characters. "The Three Billy Goats Gruff" is a simple tale with well-defined action; "Cinderella" is too long and involved for most groups. "The Elves and the Shoemaker" is an all-time favorite; "Hansel and Gretel" will be enjoyed by older children who have had many experiences with creative dramatics. The anthologies are rich sources of story material, and the reading textbooks offer many possibilities.

These steps are not presented as a formula. Some teachers may want to combine several, and some classes are more receptive and responsive than others. It is hoped that every teacher will recognize the invaluable contribution which creative play can make to the development of children and that each will proceed in her own individual way to make it an integral part of her instructional program.

five

Discussion

let's talk it over

Discussion, Fifth-Grade Style [1]

TEACHER: Most of you are playing baseball on teams in the Little League. I have heard you talking about some of the problems you encounter. Most of them seem to be concerned with behavior on or off the playing field. Let's talk about these problems. Aren't they usually related to good sportsmanship? Would some of you like to tell us about your idea of sportsmanship?

FIRST PUPIL: My idea of good sportsmanship is getting along better with other people. When you play with other people, you learn how to get along, and you also learn fair play.

SECOND PUPIL: My idea of good sportsmanship is cheering for the other team.

THIRD PUPIL: My idea of good sportsmanship is obeying one who knows better and has seen what you have done and obeying him, like, if the umpire sees that you are out and you say you weren't, you'd better obey him or he'll put you off the team.

FOURTH PUPIL: When you go to play, don't just go out there to win. You go out to lose and win and have fun and not to argue and to get along with other people.

FIFTH PUPIL: My idea is when you win a game you've got to say "Good

---

1 "Sportsmanship," a transcription of a taped discussion among the boys in the fifth-grade classroom of Mrs. Aileen Cole, Kate Shephard Elementary School, Mobile, Alabama. Used by permission.

game"—you know, when you go over there to greet him, you say "Good game" and not to yell "We won, we won" and all that. Just go over there and tell him "nice game" and "we enjoyed playing with you."

SIXTH PUPIL: In our league we play baseball and we have umpires and sometimes people get mad at the umps and the umpire tells them to be quiet or either you go sit down on the bench and not play any more of the game and sometimes when somebody's, like, stealing second, well, the guy that's playing second base goes and gets the ball and tries to tag the guy that's running and sometimes he's safe and the umpire calls him out but the umpires are not always right.

TEACHER: Do you think he's doing the best he can?

SIXTH PUPIL: Yes, ma'am because they hire the umpires to do the best they can. I think the umpires are real good. The umpires, before they can hire 'em, they have to go to umpire school and that takes a long time, so we ought to be very thankful that they even give their time to help us, so there wouldn't be a lot of arguing and fightin'.

TEACHER: When did good sportsmanship start for you today?

THIRD PUPIL: This morning when I got up out of bed. Sometimes you wake up in the mornings and you're not happy because you didn't get a good night's rest and then you go around and you get mad at people for doing nothing really.

FIFTH PUPIL: I was a bad sportsman when we were playing a game of baseball at school. I hit the ball and I got on second and then Terry Orso hit the ball and I got on third and I tried to knock John down so he'd drop the ball so I'd be safe.

TEACHER: Who did you hurt when you did that?

FIFTH PUPIL: Me.

TEACHER: Why?

FIFTH PUPIL: Well, because I was acting a bad sportsman and I should have been playing a good game instead of a bad one.

EIGHTH PUPIL: If you're not a good sportsman you'll soon get over it, I betcha, because you'll be arguing with other people and people won't like you. They won't want to go around with somebody who argues a lot.

NINTH PUPIL: You can learn good sportsmanship at home, too, because last night after we had finished supper, I went out to look at the house that they were building next door to us but that wasn't the only reason I went out because I just wanted to get away from doing the dishes because me and my brother always do the dishes but I went back in because I knew it was wrong and we did the dishes.

TENTH PUPIL: We oughta play, run, and don't fuss.

ELEVENTH PUPIL: You wouldn't have a team if everybody didn't work together.

FIFTH PUPIL: Try not to swing the bats, cause if you hit the catcher in the legs or the umpire in the legs, you might break their legs or their arms or knock them out with the bat.

TWELFTH PUPIL: When you do something wrong, the other guys on your team ought to help encourage you that you'll be able to catch it next time or something like that.

SIXTH PUPIL: It's not if you win the game, it's if you played it fairly and it's harder to be a good winner than a good loser.

FIFTH PUPIL: If somebody makes a mistake, don't yell at 'em because you might be the next one to make a mistake; just say, "That's all right. You'll do better next time."

SIXTH PUPIL: The coaches spend their time out with the boys trying to teach them how to have more fun together and when they're out teaching us how to play ball and stuff like that they could be out bowling or playing golf or something.

FIRST PUPIL: The coaches work and try to get to know you like every week you have practice. They want to get to know you better.

EIGHTH PUPIL: Never get mad at 'em because you're out there to learn from the coaches. You learn how to play ball. If you get mad you probably won't learn as much.

FIFTH PUPIL: If you lose, you're not supposed to go to the other team and tell them that they cheated, and if you win, you're not supposed to go around saying "Yea, we win."

TEACHER: Why shouldn't you do that?

FIFTH PUPIL: It's not good sportsmanship because it makes the other team feel bad. You know how you learn to be a better sportsman— like you played last year and you try to be a better sportsman the next year. If you get out and you just walk off then you know mentally you're a better sportsman.

TEACHER: Our time is almost gone. Who can sum up this discussion on good sportsmanship and keep it affirmative—keep it what we can do, not what let's don't do.

FOURTH PUPIL: Well, what we can do is we can play better, we can obey the umpire or whoever knows better than we do.

EIGHTH PUPIL: We can make up for our errors that we make.

SIXTH PUPIL: We can always play fair.

FIRST PUPIL: We can practice on not slinging our bats and how to bat better.

FIFTH PUPIL: We also can help boys who don't know how to throw real well and teach them how to throw and to catch good.

THIRD PUPIL: It's almost the end of school and I'm going to try my best to play and forget my errors.

SIXTH PUPIL: You should try your best all year long.

FIFTH PUPIL: Never get mad at the other team if they won or brag too much if you win.

NINTH PUPIL: Cause you might lose the next game and then you'll be sorry.

TEACHER: Who has a good definition of your own for good sportsmanship? Of what a good sport is?

TWELFTH PUPIL: He's a friend of others and is enjoyed by others and you can call him a sportsman.

SEVENTH PUPIL: He doesn't just like one friend. He likes everybody in the whole classroom.

TEACHER: Would anyone else like to help sum up the discussion?

THIRTEENTH PUPIL: A few months back we had an award for two of the people from our school that received a medal for being good sportsmen.

TEACHER: But they only accepted that medal. We have many good sportsmen—many children who play the game well inside and outside the classroom. They accepted it for all of us. Our time is almost gone. Who else would like to help sum up your idea of a good sport?

FOURTH PUPIL: He's also one who makes friends with everybody and he doesn't argue at 'em. He helps 'em learn how to do better and not to make the same mistake over.

SIXTH PUPIL: A good sportsman is always honest usually, too.

SEVENTH PUPIL: I think this discussion will help us to be better sportsmen, to learn better rules and to help ourselves.

TEACHER: That's a very good way to end it, Carl. Thank you so much.

The preceding transcription of a discussion which occurred in a fifth-grade class reveals a number of important aspects and characteristics of the discussion technique. First, the problem being discussed is appropriate in terms of both the age level of the children involved and the social significance of the subject. Ten-year-olds are tremendously interested in sports, and they are becoming deeply sensitive to the concepts of fair play and social justice. No one can doubt the value of sportsmanlike behavior in all areas of human endeavor, so this problem has real, inherent value. The achievement of effective classroom discussion depends, first of all, on the selection of timely, provocative topics.

A second characteristic of a good discussion is pointed up in the transcription. This is the level of involvement and attentiveness displayed by the pupils. These children are vitally interested; they have been encouraged to listen carefully; they are thinking through the various aspects of the problem; they are seeing rational relationships and making thoughtful judgments. Under such circumstances the discipline is inherent in the situation. Teachers who are concerned about the apathy and boredom found in many classrooms will find that the use of discussion presents an interesting challenge.

Third, this discussion is going some place. It moves purposefully and logically from one area to the next. The participants can feel a sense of accomplishment and completion. Most teachers are all too familiar with the futility of the aimless chattering which passes as discussion in some of our professional meetings. Children feel this same sense of frustration if their ideas are never directed and plans never consummated. Discussions must move along if they are to be effective.

The interesting flow of participation is the fourth aspect which should be considered. These fifth graders are neither talking to nor trying to impress their teacher. They are sharing *their* ideas and concerns with *their* peers and reaching *their* conclusions. This gives them a vested interest in the decisions and a basis for further study and deliberation. The flow of contributions is from participant to participant, not from participant to leader. This must be the pattern of a real discussion.

The role of the teacher as the status leader in the classroom presents the fifth element of concern. Much of the work of the teacher is done before the discussion takes place. A favorable climate is established; materials are made available; standards are set; and an outline of the main points in the form of open-ended questions may be given. When the discussion begins, the teacher becomes a group member, an observer, and a guide. The teacher of the group on the tape does not see herself as an examiner who must somehow derive a grade for each child or as the authority who has all the final answers. She serves as an interested participant who has leadership skills which are exercised when they are needed.

A major factor in the rationale for the use of the discussion technique is the level of the thought processes involved. The development of problem-solving behavior is a primary goal of modern education. The taped discussion presents ample evidence of this sixth characteristic. These pupils are using the skills of critical analysis and evaluative judgment in a functional situation. Creative contributions and divergent thinking are encouraged and treasured in a good classroom discussion.

Finally, the transcribed discussion provides for summarization and evaluation. The major points are reviewed and systematized; the final plans or decisions are outlined and clarified; and the entire proceedings are brought together into a cohesive, unified whole. Consistent with the demands of the problem-solving approach, the current discussion period is terminated but the problem area is left open for more thought and study and the gathering of further evidence. Effective discussion must effect some closure, but it must also leave the interest level at an optimum peak for further thought and effort.

Clarification of meaning

If teachers were asked to list learning activities according to frequency of use, discussion would be given a high priority. However, many of the learning situations which are labeled discussion are not that at all. Far too many of the classroom "discussions" which have been observed are merely recitations in which the teacher asks a question, a child answers, the teacher asks another question, and another child answers. The flow of discourse is from teacher to pupil throughout the period. This type of oral activity usually limits the level of the thought processes involved to memorization and recall and has none of the significant characteristics of a real discussion.

In order to promote classroom discussion it is necessary to have a clear idea of what discussion is and what it involves. According to most definitions, to *discuss* is to investigate by reasoning or argument, to present in detail, and to talk about something; frequently listed synonyms include *argue, debate,* and *dispute.* All of these involve discourse in order to reach conclusions or to convince, but there are definitive differences between these processes and discussions, and these differences need careful consideration and analysis by both teacher and pupils. A discussion of what discussion is, as well as what it is not, should take place within the classroom. The different forms of communication should be recognized and defined precisely and accurately, not improperly identified as discussion.

Authors on the subject of discussion vary slightly in their definitions, but all stress the basic idea that discussion is a form of oral group communication with a definite topic and purpose; that it involves solving problems by seeking facts, asking questions, and investigating all sides of a problem; that some conclusions based on the best evidence available are reached; and that all members of the group are involved in reaching the conclusions.

Discussion must be a vital part of the school program if the educative process is to equip the child with the skills and insights for solving his problems in a rapidly changing world. Rote answers and formal routines are simply not enough to prepare the child to live creatively and productively.

The values of discussion

In planning the instructional program and deciding on teaching techniques, teachers must be concerned both with the child as an individual and with each child as a member of a group. The use of discussion can make significant contributions in both areas. In regard to its group values Jarolimek says:

> Its value lies chiefly in the fact that it represents a type of intellectual teamwork, resting on the philosophy and principle that the pooled knowledge, ideas and feelings of several persons have greater merit than those of a single individual.[2]

A wide variety of information, opinions, ideas, and talents may be presented on a topic through the use of discussion. There is a greater likelihood of errors being discovered and corrected than when an individual works alone. As a result of sharing, combining, and evaluating ideas, the group solution of problems is quite likely to have greater depth and validity than the work of an individual.

Group members tend to become more interested, more strongly

[2] John Jarolimek, *Social Studies in Elementary Education* (New York: The Macmillan Company, 1964), p. 197.

motivated, and more involved in learning as a result of participation in discussion. This involvement leads to deeper understanding and greater possibility of changes in both attitude and behavior. Class members are also more willing and cooperative in carrying out discussions that they have had a part in making.

Discussion is a procedure which enables children to develop attitudes and skills which are appropriate to productive living in our democratic society. It provides practice and guidance in working together to solve problems and to make decisions, and it encourages commitment to those decisions.

Experiences in discussion are useful to the individual child in many ways. The child may gain the following advantages:

1. Development of the social skills that are so necessary for carrying out group work.

2. Development of more clear-cut, orderly thinking.

3. Improvement in the skills of organizing, summarizing, and evaluating.

4. Development of more effective speech habits.

5. Increase in vocabulary and the ability to express himself.

6. Development of the ability to listen carefully and purposefully.

7. Increase in the realization that most problems are complex and require objective evaluation.

8. Development of poise and composure in facing problems.

9. Increase in the ability to make decisions in a variety of life situations.

Limitations and disadvantages

Discussion revolves in a complex matrix of human relationships and ideas. As might be expected, this complexity results in certain limitations which should be recognized and examined for possible solutions.

Discussion takes a great deal of time. A flexible schedule is mandatory. Sometimes it is difficult to get a good discussion going. Planning, preparation, and experience, on the part of both the teacher and the pupils, will help solve this problem, but it is un-

Another step in the preparation for discussion is the setting up of standards regarding the desired skills, attitudes, and behaviors pertinent to the technique. The group which participated in the discussion quoted earlier had set up these *standards for discussion* soon after the term began:

1. Think before you speak.
2. One person talks at a time.
3. Listen.
4. Be polite.
5. Give everyone a chance.
6. Ask questions at a proper time.
7. Keep to the subject.

These standards have several outstanding qualities. They are stated positively; they are expressed in language natural to children; and the list is brief enough to be effective and broad enough to encompass the criteria for discussion behavior. The teacher will use the setting up of standards as an initial step in developing discussion techniques, and she and the group will refer to them as things go awry in future situations.

The topic for the discussion must be clearly defined and understood. Many discussions break down because the topic is too broad to attack, too ambiguous to be defined, or so restricted by factual or cultural determinism that the outcome is obvious from the beginning. The teacher helps ensure success through careful planning of open-ended key questions which will serve to clarify the issues and stimulate thinking. It is extremely important that these questions be thought-provoking. Questions which require only a "yes" or "no" or a one-word answer will stifle the discussion. Open-ended questions will help children develop insight into the problem so that they may continue the questioning process. These key questions may be listed on the board to serve as a guide.

Adequate time for preparation must be allowed. A discussion centered on a school-oriented problem such as the one on sportsmanship or a consideration of how to improve behavior in the lunchroom may require only a short period of concentrated thought, while a subject-matter discussion such as one dealing with framing the Constitution may need a week or more of research. Time is only one factor of preparation; availability of a wide range of materials is just as necessary. The range refers to types of materials such as textbooks, resource books, encyclopedias, periodicals, and newspapers and to levels of difficulty ranging from materials suitable for disabled readers to those intended for adult use. Discussion should not be attempted until sufficient materials are collected; in this era of proliferation of printed materials this will not present an obstacle.

One of the most useful tools which we can give children is an understanding of and efficiency in using research skills. Such skills as locating information, taking notes, outlining, and organizing should receive consistent attention from the time the table of contents is introduced in the first grade until the functional bibliography is developed in the sixth. The development of research skills in the preparation for discussion is an ideal way to make those learnings meaningful, and it offers an excellent opportunity for the integration of subjects and areas.

Children should be made aware of the different types of contributions which can help to develop more interest and depth in the discussion. Mauree Applegate lists these as follows:

1. Tell one part of what you have read—not everything the first time you contribute.
2. Add more information to something someone else has said.
3. Ask a good question.
4. Challenge a particular statement.
5. Give your own opinion and back your opinion with documented evidence.
6. Show pictures or objects which relate to the topic.[3]

A good way to help the children become familiar with the use of these techniques is to have a group demonstrate them. Afterwards, the class may identify, analyze, discuss, and evaluate the demonstration. This list, or a similar one developed by the pupils, should be put on a chart and displayed for ready reference during the initial phases of preparation.

Summarization and evaluation are important aspects of discussion. Discussion contributions should be summarized at the end

[3] Mauree Applegate, *Easy in English* (New York: Harper & Row, Publishers, 1963), pp. 171–172.

of the session and then evaluated by the group. Favorable comments as well as helpful criticism should be included. This phase of discussion is important for making improvements, and it serves as a guide for progress.

Flow charts, according to Dawson, Zollinger, and Elwell,[4] can help pupils become better aware of their part in group discussion. They illustrate the exchange of ideas between members of the group and help the class become more conscious of patterns of communication in mature discussion. Free interchange between pupil and pupil instead of only between pupil and teacher, a wide distribution of response, and use of topic-related statements are marks of good discussion and make for situations where children may practice democratic procedures and develop independent thinking.

A procedure suggested for use with older groups is the appointment of a person to serve as an observer. The observer assists the leader in helping the group to work in a democratic way. During discussion he notes whether all members participate, whether any member (including the leader) is dominating the discussion, whether some members are talking too much, and whether discussion is staying on the subject. During the evaluation period the observer reports on these matters and helps the group evaluate their progress. These observations are useful in helping the group to make specific improvements.

Questionnaire types of evaluation or listing of accomplishments and shortcomings are other methods for evaluation that might be adapted for use in the classroom to add variety and to increase insight.

As stated previously, the teacher should serve as discussion leader until the children become familiar with the techniques of discussion, when a group leader could be selected from the class. Student leaders serve to stimulate the class and help develop a stronger feeling of class responsibility.

The duties of the leader should be discussed and criteria for leadership set up and referred to before discussion. Small discussion groups offer a good opportunity for the training of student leaders. Every child should be given the opportunity to develop his abilities to lead through various group situations.

[4] Mildred A. Dawson, Marian Zollinger, and Ardell Elwell, *Guiding Language Learning* (New York: Harcourt, Brace & World, Inc., 1964), pp. 408–410.

Preoccupation with the techniques and preparation for discussion should not deter the teacher from providing a rich variety of learning experiences. Discussion is an excellent teaching-learning device, but it is only one of many. As Applegate so aptly states:

> Any method overused destroys interest; any method underused loses learning and hinders growth. Discussion is only one method of exchanging ideas, facts, and opinions.[5]

Types of discussion

Teachers overlook some worthwhile experiences by restricting discussion to the informal type which occurs when the class as a whole discusses a topic. In addition to this informal discussion, there are several other types which are very useful in the classroom.

A *round-table discussion* involves a small group of from three to eight people, including a moderator. Its purpose may be simply to share ideas or to deal with a particular problem in an informal manner. The moderator must guide the group so as to keep the discussion moving and on the topic. He helps the group summarize and evaluate results. The moderator, the members of the discussion group, and the audience, if there is one, need to have clear ideas of their responsibilities.

The entire class may be divided into small groups and each group may simultaneously engage in round-table discussion, or one group may participate while the rest of the class listens as an audience. This is the best procedure to use until the class is thoroughly familiar with round-table discussion.

The *panel discussion* is similar to the round-table discussion, but the procedure is somewhat more formal and is more audience-oriented. An audience is always present for the panel discussion and is usually allowed to ask questions and participate when the discussion between the panel members is over. Panel members have a responsibility to be more than adequately prepared for each is cast in the role of an authority on the subject.

Buzz groups constitute another type of discussion group and may be devised by dividing the class into a number of smaller sub-

[5] Applegate, *op. cit.*, p. 172.

groups of five or six members. A specific problem is given for consideration, and a limited amount of time is set for each group to arrive at an answer or a response.

Hoffman and Pluchik [6] list this as a useful technique for establishing a problem or an area for discussion, for arriving at answers to problems, and for summarizing the views of the class on some matter. It is helpful in establishing a sense of friendship between group members, and, because it is less formal than most types of discussion, it encourages the shy students to participate. Buzz groups are flexible devices which may be adapted and modified in many different situations.

Buzz groups may get out of hand and result in little more than wasted time unless clearly understood ground rules are laid in advance. The children need to keep their purpose firmly in mind and proceed in accomplishing their purpose with as little noise and confusion as possible.

Brainstorming is a way of getting a great many ideas from a group on a particular problem and is regarded as being a good means of releasing group creativity. This technique is based on four simple rules which must be followed for good results:

1. No idea may be criticized, evaluated, or rejected during the brainstorming.

2. All ideas are acceptable regardless of how improbable they may seem.

3. Emphasis is placed on quantity of suggestion.

4. Group members may add to, combine, or improve the ideas of others.

This is a stimulating and useful technique for solving problems of discovery, but, as Harnack and Fest [7] indicate, its effectiveness is limited to those problems that are specific, simple, and familiar and to those that involve discovering solutions; it is not effective in evaluating or choosing between solutions.

Role playing is a form of creative dramatics which is very effective in encouraging children to think and to better understand

[6] Randall W. Hoffman and Robert Pluchik, *Small-group Discussion in Orientation and Teaching* (New York: G. P. Putnam's Sons, 1959), p. 61.

[7] R. Victor Harnack and Thorrel B. Fest, *Group Discussion: Theory and Technique* (New York: Appleton-Century-Crofts, 1964), pp. 83–84.

another person's problem or point of view. Role playing helps children to explore and develop different ways of solving problems. It is valuable in solving problems concerning human relationships and is very effective in helping children to develop a sense of involvement in problems of history. "Most important of all, children learn from role-playing that live issues always have at least two sides." [8]

Role playing should be thought of as a means of presenting a specific situation for class discussion. The dramatic action should be cut before the problem has been solved so that the group can speculate on and analyze the problem. The teacher should be prepared to ask questions which would trigger discussion and evaluation.

Role playing should start with a simple problem, spontaneity should be encouraged, and too much personal involvement should be discouraged. Insight and understanding may be further developed by having the actors reverse their roles; this reversal produces a new approach to the problem. Role playing should be based on a knowledge of the subject under consideration. It should be used only after wide reading and research. It should be emphasized that role playing is not designed to amuse, and, as with other methods, it should not be used too often.

These different types of discussion are valuable to the classroom because they add variety, create interest, increase motivation, and fill specific needs. Small-group discussion situations help each individual to become more actively involved and to become a better participant. The shy child will feel freer to volunteer information in the informal atmosphere of the buzz group. Confidence, practice, and skill may be acquired by the child in the small group which will enable him to function better when the class as a unit has discussions.

With good panel discussion the class audience has the opportunity to observe discussion processes. The fact that they are not actively involved helps them to be more objective in their observation, analysis, and evaluation. Such observations increase their ability to participate in meaningful discussion.

[8] Applegate, *op. cit.,* p. 67.

The beginning, the middle, and the end

Many teachers become discouraged with the use of classroom discussion because their efforts never seem to "pay off" in terms of increasing skill or complexity. Many times this is the result of lack of provision for the sequential nature of its development. Conversation and discussion are not the same thing at all, but the "show and tell" time in the first-grade classroom is a beginning point in sharing ideas and information. It can be used as a springboard to real discussion.

One first-grade teacher used the toys brought to school after Christmas to initiate a unit on simple tools which resulted in discussion on a rather sophisticated level. When Timmy showed his dump truck, the teacher asked, "How does it work?" The concepts of the inclined plane, the pulley, and the lever were developed from examination of the various toys. Examples of the use of these principles in accomplishing the work of the world were identified. By the time the children had worked with films, pictures, and visitors who came in to explain and demonstrate various tools they had enough information and experience to make real discussion possible.

Another teacher used the narcissus bulbs brought in by an interested mother to develop a study of the conditions necessary for plant growth. The result was a beautiful spring garden of tulips, daffodils, anemones, and hyacinths, but the children became quite accustomed to "researching" catalogs and books and were highly motivated to share their information. A second grade had a similar experience when their new aquarium had to be set up.

The point is that discussion must begin on a very simple level and progress to the subject-matter discussions expected in the upper grades. If older children have not had sharing experiences, some provision for the less difficult exchange of ideas must be made. Pronovost suggests that specific lessons should be used to emphasize discussion skills and attitudes in the following sequence:

1. *a.* Desire to contribute to the discussion.
   b. Willingness to listen to the others' points of view.
2. *a.* Ability to stick to the topic of discussion while giving evidence to support one's point of view.

    b. Ability to listen for supporting evidence related to main topic of discussion.

    3. Ability to organize one's thoughts in speaking and listening according to a problem-solving pattern of definition, analysis, exploration, evaluation, and decision.

    4. Ability to serve as a teacher or follow leadership in a discussion.

    5. Ability to participate in meetings conducted according to parliamentary procedures.[9]

Teachers may devise "case studies" centered on one of the items for the children to consider. Discussions on television, tape, or phonograph records may be used to illustrate a particular skill. Written exercises dealing with the identification of major points and substantiating points may be used occasionally.

Some very effective teachers like to start with having pupils talk about areas of daily school living. Such topics as the duties of the student council, requirements for election to the safety patrol, behavior in the library, or the use of the cafeteria have the advantages of requiring little research and preparation time and of being of immediate concern to group members.

Whatever the approach chosen, teachers must remember that the development of discussion skills follows the same pattern as that of other developmental skills, proceeding always from the simple to the complex. Only a relatively few adults possess all the insights, attitudes, and skills in human relations requisite for effective participation in a worthwhile discussion. It follows that we must allow children time and opportunity for progress.

Good classroom discussion is neither simple nor easy to achieve. There are a number of helpful guidelines but no set rules which will guarantee success and assure satisfactory results. Certainly the advantages and benefits to both the individual pupil and the class as a group make it a worthwhile object of our best efforts and a valuable method of learning.

---

[9] Wilbur Pronovost with Louise Kingman, *The Teaching of Speaking and Listening* (New York: David McKay Company, Inc., 1961), p. 175.

six

Reporting

now i'll tell you about . . .

Teddy was seven years old. With all the aplomb of a Dale Carnegie graduate, he stood before his class and told how the use of the inclined plane has made man's work easier. He used some of his toys (a dump truck, an auto transport truck, and a railroad freight car and ramp) to illustrate the uses of an inclined plane. Then he used various objects (a metal ball, a plastic horse, and a small car) to demonstrate to his first-grade listeners that it is easier to roll or push an object up a gradual slope than to lift it from one level to another.

Several fifth graders were assigned a group report on the Middle Atlantic states. A well-defined criterion for the reports had been established, but the group was allowed to choose the method of presentation. They decided to present a skit which revolved around "David's" difficulties in trying to prepare an unreasonable assignment for a harsh teacher. As he worked to finish in one night a report on all the Middle Atlantic states, David fell asleep. In his troubled dreams, each state appeared to give all the pertinent information about itself. As each state presented his report, the others helped him hold maps, charts, and pictures which had been prepared to illustrate the talks.

Dale, a sixth grader, used an overhead projector to add interest and visual reinforcement to his report on the planetary system. He spoke of the orbital path of each planet and its size and distance from the sun and showed a transparency to illustrate these points. Then he described each planet and used a chart for each to point out unique characteristics. He and his classmates had made the transparencies. They were carefully scaled, colorfully portrayed, and neatly labeled. Dale closed his report with a poised, "Do you have any questions?" and proceeded to answer several. In response to one question concerning the possibility of undiscovered planets, he promised further research and a report on his findings the following day.

These anecdotes describe oral reporting at its best. Certainly it is not difficult to hear it at its worst in classrooms all over the country. Difficulties and discouragement with this technique are a frequently voiced concern of teachers. So the purpose here is to present an analysis of the characteristics of reporting and of its values and pitfalls. Finally, specific suggestions for the development of effective oral reports are included to help teachers in the optimum use of this valuable oral activity.

Characteristics and opportunities

Some of the characteristics of good reporting parallel those of discussion. Reports are used when there is a real need for information and ideas. The topics should be appropriate to the developmental level of the children and geared to the interests of the speaker and the listeners. As with the discussion technique, the subject matter should be significant to the objectives of some phase of the instructional program, and the report should be directed toward answering questions, solving problems, or expanding concepts.

There is, however, one critical difference between reporting and discussion which is frequently overlooked or minimized. It is possible to carry on a good discussion with one or two ineffective people in the group. This is not true in reporting. The reporter is on his own! No one else can pick up the ball and carry it. This makes for added complexity and imposes several responsibilities on the child and his teacher. The added responsibilities include:

1. Greater specificity in the choice of the subject.

2. More depth in the research on the topic.
3. More skill in the organization of the material.
4. More attention to the time element.
5. Greater language facility.
6. More poise and assurance in the speaking situation.

Preparing and giving a report is a mature learning activity which requires a large complex of skills and abilities. The sequential development of these skills presents a great challenge to the teacher, but the many opportunities and needs for using reporting and the educational values of this activity more than justify her efforts.

The ability to report is a versatile tool which is required in many classroom situations. This is only a partial listing of its many areas of use:

1. To present information on a specific topic in a subject-matter area.
2. To describe a personal experience—a trip, a concert, or a play, for example.
3. To summarize or explain a project or an experiment.
4. To make announcements concerning school activities or policies.
5. To share current events.
6. To give directions for playing games or for construction activities.
7. To give reports on school organization meetings attended in the capacity of class representative.
8. To share books and articles.
9. To present information derived from interviews or radio or television programs.
10. To summarize the plans or findings of group activities.

Values and limitations

Oral reporting has many of the communicative values attributed to the other oral activities discussed here, but, because it is an individual activity, it also has some values which are unique. Anyone who has ever given a successful report can attest to the warm glow of self-satisfaction which is generated. Few other activities can compare in the development of feelings of adequacy and competence. The reinforcement from an interested, receptive audience and the favorable comments of its members can make an invaluable contribution to the self-concept of the speaker.

By the same token, no greater damage to one's self-image may accrue than that suffered in some reporting situations. Jarolimek describes such a situation quite graphically:

> There is nothing quite so deadly or lacking in instructional value as the elementary child giving a "report" he has copied from the encyclopedia. He stumbles over every other word because he neither knows its meaning nor how to pronounce it. Because he must ask for help in reading his report, it lacks continuity, is hard to follow, and is not understood by the class. The listeners cannot follow what the child is attempting to present, become bored and/or disruptive. Under such a set of circumstances no one likes to give reports or listen to them. They are a waste of time.[1]

They are worse than a waste of time. A child who has faced such a frustrating, belittling experience is unlikely to ever feel quite comfortable about himself and his capabilities or to seek participation in other oral activities.

The individual nature of reporting also gives pupils opportunities to explore individual interests and to exploit their own experiences. In this activity the bright child may go off on the intellectual jaunts he needs so urgently and the slow learner can experience success because he can work with materials and ideas at his own level of achievement.

Here, again, the "oneness" quality occasions a word of caution. Traditionally, teachers prefer group activities, but, having experienced the values described above, some may tend to overwork the reporting technique. Too many reports given too frequently can be devastating to the interest level of the students and to the learning outcomes of the instructional program. There are other effective ways of providing for the wide range of abilities and interests found in any group of learners.

[1] John Jarolimek, *Social Studies in Elementary Education*, third edition (New York: The Macmillan Company, 1967), pp. 221–222.

The current emphasis on the need for systematic instruction on the research and organization skills points up another important value of reporting. Much too often these skills are taught out of context as a separate, isolated lesson. Since they are prerequisite to the preparation of a report, the children have a real purpose in learning how to choose and locate materials, how to identify main and substantiating ideas, how to outline, and how to make and use notes.

The ability to make decisions and the quality of adaptability are defensible goals of education. Good reporting demands the ability to "think on one's feet." Decisions concerning time limitations, the interest level of the audience, and the suitability of certain ideas must be made quickly as the report moves along. Adjustments in length and content are usually necessary, some points being deleted and others elaborated upon. These demands help the reporters on their way to mature decision making and flexibility of reaction.

General suggestions

Here are six general guidelines which may be helpful to teachers who want to include reporting in their repertoire of teaching strategies. These cut across all grade and age levels; they are as significant to the six-year-old talking about the care of his pet as to the sixth grader giving his findings on the fuels for space crafts.

The first one refers to the establishment of purpose. The child needs to know the exact dimensions of his topic, what kinds of information it should include, and how it fits in with the reports of classmates and with the general area of study. Children are prone to bite off too large a chunk in choosing a subject, and the teacher's words of caution are not enough. A teacher–pupil conference is the best way to help the pupil delimit his subject and think through his major points of emphasis.

The development of a clear understanding of what is expected in the reporting situation is the second area of concern. Many teachers like to have their groups work out standards charts. A fifth-grade teacher had three. One began with "When we prepare our reports . . . ," the second with "When we give our reports . . . ," while the third was developed to point up the responsibilities of the audience: "When we listen to reports. . . ." Again, standards charts should result from the thinking of the group, should be worded positively, and should be removed before children look at them without seeing them. They can be posted again when the need for referral arises.

The third responsibility is the provision of adequate materials and instruction in their use. Encyclopedias, atlases, periodicals, and many informative books at all represented levels of reading ability should be readily available. Availability, however, is no guarantee of effective use. Several sixth graders, each with a different volume, were turning pages in the encyclopedia. They told an observer that they were looking for "stuff about Abraham Lincoln." Further investigation revealed that one or two didn't know that such books are alphabetized; none of them knew about the index or cross references. Does this seem impossible? If every teacher assumes that the preceding teacher has taught certain skills, it is quite possible. Skillful teachers make no such assumptions. They check for levels of skill development and provide needed instruction or review.

The fourth guideline is the need to help children add interest and spice to the reports through the use of many audiovisual devices. Pictures, maps, globes, graphs, and charts can be used to sustain interest and to expand concepts. Hand puppets are excellent props when impersonations or simulated interviews are appropriate to the subject. The use of flannelboards, magnetic boards, and overhead and opaque projectors gives visual reinforcement to the spoken word. Roller movies, slides, and filmstrips give emphasis and depth. An occasional tape-recorded report will be a challenge to the speaker and a novelty to the listeners. All of these devices may be used by elementary-school students if they have seen the teacher use them and if they have had help in their operation and use. These have another value, too; they tend to give the speaker added self-confidence.

Making provision for practice of the report is the fifth suggestion. It is probably safe to say that no report should be given before it is rehearsed at least once. Sometimes the child practices on his own. Here the tape recorder is a valuable aid. He may be encouraged to seek the help of his parents, or pairs of children may practice on each other. All of these are valuable, but none of them can accomplish quite as much as rehearsing before the teacher. At least once each child should experience the values of this one-to-one relationship. The teacher then has the opportunity to praise, to encourage, to offer suggestions, to note language and speech difficulties, and to develop the warm interpersonal relationship that is so vital to effective teaching.

Finally, the problem of evaluation must be considered. A comprehensive treatment of this subject in relation to all types of oral activities makes up the bulk of the final chapter. Two suggestions concerning evaluation of the child's report seem appropriate here. First, the child's first experiences with reporting must be successful. He must feel good about himself and his contribution. So the criticism is positive! Choose his major strength to comment on and use it to start building greater skill. Second, when weaknesses are identified, work on one at a time. Children become discouraged and teachers frustrated when they attempt to improve speech patterns, sentence structure, organization of material, and language usage in one lesson.

Planning for sequential development

The establishment of sequence in all areas of the instructional program is a major concern of curriculum makers and teachers. It is especially difficult for such a complex skill as reporting, where it seems that a number of related skills must be developed and synthesized at one time. The following suggestions are offered with the full realization that a blueprint of teaching procedure is often unrealistic and restrictive. Some teachers may want to move more rapidly; others may teach children who need many preliminary opportunities in less complex forms of oral communication. And all teachers will want to modify the program in terms of their own experiences and creative ideas.

The six steps in preparing and giving a report may be categorized in this manner:

1. Choosing and delimiting a topic in terms of
   a. the interest of the pupil and the needs of the group,
   b. the information available,
   c. the maturity of the reporter and time allotment.

2. Determining the purpose so that the child understands whether
   he is
   a. giving information,
   b. proving a point,
   c. explaining an experiment or a theory.
3. Establishing the major idea according to
   a. the reporter's viewpoint,
   b. a specific idea proposed in the reference material.
4. Collecting information from
   a. one or more reference books, using the table of contents and
      the index,
   b. the encyclopedia, using the index and cross-references,
   c. a card catalog, using subject and author listings,
   d. files of pictures, charts, brochures, pamphlets, and clippings.
5. Organizing information according to bibliography cards with
   a. a card for each source,
   b. author, title, publisher, and date of publication on each
      card,
   c. notes written in pupils' own words.
6. Presenting the report with
   a. an interesting introduction,
   b. devices to provide visual reinforcement,
   c. acceptable language usage,
   d. a tight cohesive organizational pattern,
   e. good voice and speaking qualities,
   f. a strong, vigorous conclusion.

Even a cursory examination of this demanding process will
reveal the developmental nature of reporting. Obviously young
children cannot (and should not be expected to) cope with many
of these tasks. Teachers working with the six- and seven-year-olds
will want to keep their learning objectives simple, the occasions for
reporting informal, and the time allotment brief. Defensible areas
for concentrated effort are:

1. The need to speak so that everyone can hear.
2. The need to stick to the subject.
3. The need to tell events or ideas in sequence.
4. The development of larger and more colorful vocabularies.

Young children may be expected to talk one or two minutes on events coming out of their own experiences: their pets, parties, vacations, foods, and holidays. They also enjoy making announcements of school events, and they like to report on some aspect of a field trip, a science project, or a simple social concept. They should be encouraged to use pictures, toys, experiments, and flannelboards to illustrate their talks.

Teachers who work with the third and fourth graders should capitalize on the tremendous curiosity and drive of the eight- and nine-year-olds to help them make real progress in their reporting skills. They are quite capable of identifying main points, and many of them can make simple outlines. They like to use tables of contents and indexes to investigate several sources of information, and they can synthesize and compare ideas. Assistance in using the encyclopedia appeals to their sense of growing up, and their strong identification with the "gang" occasions great interest in group preparation of roller movies, puppets, and flannelboard cutouts to illustrate their reports. This characteristic also explains their enjoyment in researching new games and reporting on the game strategies and rules and regulations. Other suitable topics for the middle-grade children include summaries of group activities in science and social studies, book reports, and reports on the significance and construction of model airplanes, cars, ships, and forts.

The fifth and sixth graders have built-in antennas attuned to the big world in which they're beginning to feel they have a place. Their needs for competence and achievement are prevalent. They want to *know*, and they are more willing and more capable of working independently than younger children are. During these years teachers should stress the research skills: the basics of using the Dewey decimal system (that is, the use of the card catalog) and, for some children, the *Reader's Guide to Periodical Literature*. The ten- and eleven-year-olds must have instruction in how to skim for pertinent information, how to make notes, and how to write and use bibliography cards. They can deal effectively with outlining, so their reports have greater depth and more detail. The range of appropriate topics is as wide as the curriculum. Their strivings for identification make reports on "heroes" especially interesting. Interest in sports offers another area; stirring of social consciousness and concern for fair play opens up topics in the social sciences. The

budding scientists in these grades have real purpose in the preparation of reports in science, and since the students will be actively
involved in school organizations, they need opportunities to report
on these. The upper-grade children can make their own charts,
graphs, and maps, and they are challenged and intrigued with the
use of film projectors, overhead projectors, and tape recorders.

The development of reporting skills is a demanding, time-
consuming task, but the contributions to the child's intellectual
growth, to his capacity to handle new and difficult ideas, and to his
ability to communicate these ideas more than justifies the teacher's
time and effort. Don M. Wolfe puts it this way:

> The more often each boy and girl in the class can rise, come forward,
> face the class, and speak even a few sentences on a prepared topic, the
> more certain he is to acquit himself well in the hundreds of occasions
> to come.[2]

2 Don M. Wolfe, *Language Arts and Life Patterns* (New York: The Odyssey
Press, Inc., 1961), pp. 351–352.

seven
Using children's literature
once upon a time . . .

Children's literature offers treasures more valuable than the pot of gold at the end of the rainbow, miracles unsurpassed by Aladdin's famous lamp, and variety unrivaled by the colors of Joseph's coat. Children's books are a veritable storehouse of stimulating educational experiences. The first and second graders who are the speakers on the following transcribed tape of an unrehearsed sharing period are revealing much more than an amazing knowledge of authors and illustrators. They are experiencing reading in the most meaningful sense, and they are using the experience to develop valuable oral communication skills.

Book Sharing, Second-Grade Style [1]

I like Robert McCloskey's book, *One Morning in Maine*. On the first page it starts, the light is coming right down like that. Here's the picture that I like because Sal's little sister, she spilt some milk and the cat came to lap it up. And Robert McCloskey, he always makes the mouths look like the people are really talking.

I like Robert McCloskey, too, in *Make Way for Ducklings* and it won the Caldecott award. I like it because it's got good pictures in it. Every

---

[1] From a transcription of a taped book-sharing period in the first- and second-grade classroom of Sister Thaddeus, St. Pius Elementary School, Mobile, Alabama. Used by permission.

time Mr. Mallard found a place for them to live in, Mrs. Mallard said there might be foxes in the woods or turtles in the water so they kept flying and flying so then they were so tired that they couldn't fly any further. So then they flew over the Charles River. So they stayed there and made the nest. Then one day the eggs hatched out. First came Jack, then came Pack, and then came Lack, then came Mack, then came Nack, then came Quack, and then came Kack. I love all the names he gives 'em. He gives 'em rhyming names 'cause they're twins like.

I like *Time of Wonder* because it's by Robert McCloskey, too. And there's several descriptions in here that I would like to read to you. Here's one of them that makes you taste it. "Out on the islands that poke their rocky shores above the waters of Penobscot Bay, you can watch the time of the world go by from minute to minute, hour to hour, from day to day, season to season. You can watch a cloud peep over the Camden Hills thirty miles away across the bay—see it slowly grow and grow as it comes nearer and nearer. See it darken the hills with its shadow and then see it darken all the island in between." I love that description because it makes you see the storm begin.

This is Beim's book and it's *Too Many Sisters* and I like it because it's funny and it was about this boy, he had four sisters. And one morning when he was walking down the stairs he jumped over some jacks and he tumbled over a doll and he sat in a chair and there were knitting needles in it and he ran around the room and he was real mad and one day his sisters helped him and he said, "My sisters aren't so bad after all."

This is another book by Beim and it's *Kid Brother*. One day they were having a school play and Buz was the first one dancing. And his feathers fell off when he was dancing real fast and then when Frankie saw that it was his brother he picked 'em up and gave 'em to Buz and Buz thought that was being real kind and from then on he always played with Frankie every day.

I like C. W. Anderson 'cause he writes about cowboys and I like cowboys. I've read all his books and here's a description I like in *Blaze and the Gypsies*. "One day they were going at a swift gallop along the road, pretending they were in a race. Max could hardly keep up with them." I like the pictures the way they look real and really active real, too.

I like C. W. Anderson's books and all the Blaze ones. C. W. Anderson puts how to be kind in 'em. I don't like 'em 'cause they all begin the same and they all have black and white pictures. You need some colored ones.

I like C. W. Anderson because he wrote *Linda and the Indians* and it makes me feel like it was me, and it made me feel kind of frightened, too, for a moment because when the big fierce dog came she thought it looked like a wolf and it made me scared, too.

Another one that Golden McDonald wrote and Weisgard illustrated is *Little Lost Lamb*. I like the bright pictures in it. The little lamb always goes frisking off by himself and back here where they go looking for him the twilight and you can hardly see the mountain lion that's going to attack the little lamb but the boys get there in time and get him. I like it because it has a happy ending and I like happy endings.

I like *Little Island* when the wind is blowing the grass and the spider webs and it looks good. And here's the description: "Morning was quiet on the island with only the spiders swinging their webs against a gentle wind."

I like *Curious George* by Rey and I like the part when he was always curious. One day he forgot to be curious and he was real good.

I like Curious George because he's funny and he's always getting into trouble and putting his nose in other people's business. And he's always getting into trouble because he's so curious.

Dash and Dart is by Mary and Conrad Buff. It's about animals in the forest. Dash grew up to be a big buck and Dart grew up to be a doe. And this describes September: "Nights are getting cold. The trees are turning yellow. The meadow grasses are dying. The wild flowers are fading. The soft white snow is falling in the mountains. Snow is new to Dash and Dart. They have not seen snow before. Their thin brown legs shiver with cold. They do not like snow. Their mother does not like it either. It is cold." There are lots of other descriptions and they are beautiful descriptions and pictures. The pictures are of beautiful trees and waterfalls and they are beautiful.

I like *Forest Boat* because it's by Mary and Conrad Buff, too, and it's like *Dash and Dart,* too, because it tells about Dash and Dart and all the animals that live in the forest. And in *Dash and Dart* it says that Dash is going to become the king of the forest like Old Horn, and he did.

I like Mary and Conrad Buff when it rained a whole bunch and when all the animals came to get a drink.

I like Tresselt's books and his books are illustrated by Duvoisin. This is one and the name of it is *I Saw the Sea Come In* and it's a real good story. It's about a little boy and he goes out on the sea real early in the morning; "while the soft grey fog still hung in the sky, a little boy went down to the sea." And he dug there and then he walked down a little bit and found some shells and then he walked a little bit further down and then a big wave came in and he walked real far down then, and he thought he was the first one down there before he walked down and then he saw umbrellas, umbrellas, umbrellas, umbrellas, and people and people and people and then he saw the sea come in. This little boy must have been a real little boy because he built a sand castle and a big boy wouldn't build a sand castle like that. And, oh yes, he ended it by writing his name on the sand. I like the pictures in the book because he's changing from blue and white and black to colors, and blue and white and black to colors. He has that every other time.

I like Tresselt's books because some of 'em are good and this is one I like. It's illustrated by Duvoisin and written by Alvin Tresselt. And the name of it is *The Mitten*. I like all the little animals in this because first the little animal comes and then they get bigger and bigger and then a boy comes and then a big worst of all bear, he comes in and then a little ladybug comes in and before she even gets one foot in, "pop" goes all the seams, rip and pop goes the mitten. I think it is a hilarious book because it's real funny.

White Snow, Bright Snow is by Tresselt and it's illustrated by Duvoisin, and he's the one that won the Caldecott award for making the beautiful pictures because he lets you look straight into the houses when they're telling about 'em. And I like his coloring and all the snow he makes, too.

I like *Mr. Billy's Garden* and it's by Berta and Elmer Hader and I think they are husband and wife. And one illustrates it and the other does the writing. And the story is about a man and the rabbits and all the animals are always coming and getting in his garden and he goes complaining to his wife. One time he made a scarecrow and that scared them for awhile, but then one flew over and then the rest flew over and that made him furious. He ran so hard that he sprung his ankle and had to stay in bed all summer long. And he was lonely all the time because his wife had to do all the work. She couldn't come in there all the time so she put up a feeder for the birds so he could watch them and it wouldn't make him lonely. And one time there was this quail family and they was coming and he was so happy he got out of bed and he ran and he fell while he tried to get the crumbs but they got 'em and then after a little bit it was his birthday and he got a new gun. He heard on the radio that it was time to go hunting so he went hunting. And then he saw quail and quail and quail so he got ready and was going to fire his gun and almost before he could do it all the quail circled around him and that was the ones that he fed all summer long and then he tucked his gun under his arm and then he walked home and the quail followed him. That night Mr. Billy hung his new gun over the mantle over the fireplace. Then he hurried to scatter crumbs and seeds over the lawn. Rabbit was in the clover patch eating his breakfast. Mrs. Billy smiled as she poured the coffee. "Next year," she said, "I will help you plant a garden big enough for all of us."

I like *The Mighty Hunter* by Hader because the pictures look real and so do the people in 'em. And I like the queer writing and the animals can talk and I like that. I like the part when Little Brave Horn met a great big grizzly bear and he said, "I'm gonna shoot him," so he took aim and the bear said, "Why shoot me? I'm just huntin' for fun and I'm hungry right now," and so Little Brave Horn he dropped his bow and arrow and he ran and he said, "I'll never go huntin' again. I'll stay in school." I love that part and I'd like to go huntin' instead of going to school, and be like that little Indian boy.

I like Leo Politi because he writes real good books and he draws beautiful pictures. *Song of the Swallows* won the Caldecott award for being one of the best picture books and I like his descriptions. This is one I like: "On his way to school and on his way home Juan liked to look at the flowers in the mission garden. They were so gay against the old walls. Julian was also the gardener of the mission. He took much pride in showing Juan the plants because he knew and loved each one of them. Because he gave them such good care they grew strong and bore bright fragrant flowers."

I like Jack Keats's *On a Snowy Day* when Peter picks up a snowball and puts it in his pocket for tomorrow and then when he goes in for bed he checks and sees if it's still there but it's not there. And then he dreams that night that the snow had all melted and then when he woke up it hadn't and the stream was all covered up. He couldn't see a thing but the snow.

I like *Whistle for Willie* and it's also by Jack Keats. And I liked it when he always tried to whistle and one day he saw a carton at the end of the street and he got behind it and he tried to whistle and he couldn't so the dog just trotted on by and the other time he tried so hard to whistle that this time he let out a big loud whistle and the dog looked all around and he jumped out from behind the carton and he went home with the dog and showed his mother how he could whistle.

I'm talking about *John Henry* and I don't like *John Henry* because I don't think there's no such thing as a person being born with a hammer in his hand and dying with a hammer in his hand and I think that he puts too much color in his pictures and, anyway, I like stories that are true.

I like Charlotte Zolotov, because I like those blue pictures that she puts in and lots of birds and I like how she describes the birds going south.

I like Charlotte Zolotov when she wrote the *Rabbit Who Found Easter*. When he found a girl rabbit and they got married, they went back to the place where they first met and then they went back up the trail to the first part and they had babies and they lived happily ever after.

I don't like one of Dr. Seuss's books so much because he puts in the same colors all the time. Like in *The Sneetches* there's a story called the Zacks and he puts in blue and yellow all the way through and he makes up words that aren't really real.

I like Dr. Seuss's books because he makes funny words and that makes the books even funnier, and he puts in funny pictures and in the front there's a picture that I like because it's got the boy and he—this is the picture I like in *The King's Stilts*. It's a picture of the king. He's taking a bath and he has to sign all the pictures because he's busy all day long.

I don't like Dr. Seuss because he gives the children bad ideas like in *The Cat in the Hat* and they'll have nightmares with all those silly animals he puts in. He teaches 'em how to mess up a house and not clean it up after 'em. And his first books are better than his last books because the story is better. Because *The Cat in the Hat* it was written later and it's sillier, and it gives 'em ideas. But the first ones, like *Five Hundred Hats* and *The Grinch that Stole Christmas* and *The King's Stilts* and all those—I like those very much.

The teacher talks about books

Fortunate, indeed, is the teacher who has discovered the wonderland of personal enjoyment to be found in children's literature.

The literary quality is generally excellent, far surpassing that of many adult works. Many authors of children's books have developed unique styles and fine characterization. The themes are frequently provocative; the plots are interesting and challenging. Rereading one's own childhood favorites will disclose new insights and values, and many of the more recent publications are just too good to be missed.

Then the teacher can share these books with the youngsters. At times she will want to go through the entire book, telling or reading the story as she shows and comments on the illustrations. This seems to be the usual procedure in the primary grades. Upper-grade teachers frequently read a chapter or an episode each day from the longer books written for older children. These procedures certainly have value, but they are by no means the only way of generating enthusiasm for reading.

The encouragement of reading as a worthy use of leisure time is widely accepted as a defensible educational objective. The teacher can use book sharing as a means of whetting the reading appetites of boys and girls. First, as has been implied, she must *know* a great many books; second, she must be enthusiastic about them. Then she can say, "I've just read the most interesting book about a very brave little girl who jumped off a ship because her little brother had been left behind. Let me read you the part which tells about her battle with the wild dogs. If you think it is as exciting as I do, one of you may take it to the library and check it out." Or she may tell or read the funniest part: "Who ever heard of an elephant sitting on a bird's egg?"

Another stimulating experience involves reading a very explicit descriptive passage and letting the pupils draw their own interpretation. Tell them that the illustrator has drawn a very lovely picture, and, when their pictures are finished, they may see the one in the book and compare. Descriptions of characters engaging in a specific activity may be read and then drawn by the children. Be sure to give them enough background so that they have a framework of time, place, season, etc., on which to base an illustration.

The children speaking on the tape have paid particular attention to illustration. Development of aesthetic reaction and appreciation seems very important in an automated, technological age. Sharing books through directing attention to the line, color, texture, and action in the pictures can be very rewarding. Remember the child who said he liked Robert McCloskey's pictures because the people looked like they were really talking. He, and other children, will also like the personification in the illustrations of the animal characters in Robert Lawson's *Rabbit Hill* and *Ben and Me.* They'll probably want to read *White Snow, Bright Snow,* too, when they have looked at the childlike simplicity of Duvoisin's colorful drawings.

Teachers who are initiating social studies or science units may want to share a number of books related to the units. Pointing out specific areas covered by each book, summarizing the major points of interest, or showing particular diagrams, charts, or pictures will help the students with their research and create interest in the subject and in reading.

The values of the teacher's sharing her knowledge of books are many.

1. Enthusiasm is contagious: Children catch love of reading from teachers who are carriers of the interest. Reading is fun; it is also a fulfilling agent in the process of becoming a self-actualizing individual. And love of reading is *learned* just as surely as the process of reading is—from skilled teachers who know and appreciate its remarkable contribution to living.

2. Hearing about the people, places, and situations in books enlarges the child's "life space." The movement from the egocentric world of the young child toward the social consciousness and concern of the mature adult is extremely complex, and some of the steps must be taken vicariously. Knowledge of books is a significant factor.

3. The teacher's discourse serves as a model for acceptable language usage, good speech patterns, and habits and precise word choice. The sharing situation has built-in interest. Children listen, and they form impressions which enable them to emulate the speech skills of the teacher.

4. The ability to make wise choices is an important goal for education. The child's selectivity is expanded and improved through exposure to a variety of good books. He will be guided toward a more mature and discriminating literary appreciation if he learns about books through a pleasant, meaningful activity.

There is one little mechanical matter which may improve the

sharing period. This is the manner in which the book is held. It has been noted that many teachers hold the book directly in front of them and about chest high. This makes turning pages difficult and reading impossible for them. The book should be held over to the left side with the left hand curved around the far lower corner and the right hand holding the near edge near the middle. This position enables the teacher to see the illustrations, to read whatever part she likes and to turn the pages smoothly and easily without losing eye contact with the children. The pupils will find this technique helpful when it's their turn to talk about books.

Children share their favorites

Children should have many opportunities to talk about the books which they have enjoyed. They will become more personally involved in reading if they are encouraged to share their own reactions, and the sharing situations provide for many worthwhile language experiences. Here, again, the usual practice of merely telling about the stories has merit, but, with the guidance of skilled teachers, better educative experiences are possible.

The teacher may start by emphasizing the episodic element. She may ask students to identify the event which is the turning point, or climax, of the story. Or she may offer a choice between such introductory statements as:

1. The most exciting part was when _____.
2. I laughed when I read _____.
3. I was frightened when _____.
4. _____ [book character] was sad when _____.
5. The scariest part of this mystery story was _____.

In addition to requiring critical rethinking of the story, this technique has the advantage of limiting the child's presentation. Anyone who has heard a youngster rambling on and on as he tries to relate every detail will appreciate this limitation.

The children who spoke on the tape presented at the beginning of this chapter were keenly aware of the illustrations in the books they read. This awareness doesn't just happen; it must be developed. Children need to be shown that the illustrations contribute to and expand the story. They also need help in building sensitivity to fine art, and the lovely pictures in many books for children are a logical place to start. So the teacher may encourage sharing books on the basis of their illustrations. At various times, groups may want to concentrate on analyzing color, line, action, and expression.

Another element worthy of concentration is characterization. Authors work hard to create storybook people who are consistent and convincing. Good readers identify their own traits or those of their acquaintances in these characters. Discussions of characterization help children to develop understanding of human behavior and are of significant value in expanding and enriching vocabulary. Children may receive needed guidance and structure from such suggestions as:

1. Describe the character you would like as your best friend.
2. What character would you like to have along on a camping trip?
3. My favorite storybook pet is _____.
4. The character I like least of all is _____.

Students in the upper grades may reach a level of sophistication that will enable them to share information and reactions regarding theme and style in their favorite books. Too few readers recognize the theme of a book. The plot usurps the entire interest of the reader, and he fails to perceive the author's message. Themes dealing with social equality, justice, societal change, humaneness, etc., are well worth the attention of young people and should be identified. Depth reading also requires a knowledge and appreciation of such stylistic elements as literary devices, poetic prose, unusual word choice, tone, and mood. Advanced readers will enjoy sharing sessions centered on identification of theme and style.

Book reports

This writer has had the interesting experience of asking many college students about their memories of required written book reports during their school days and at seeing the question infallibly

There are no barriers between the teller and the hearer. Thi
one-to-one relationship, completely lacking in academic di
or status differentiation. It is a relaxed situation which en
ges release of tension. The laughter, the anticipation, th
fication with people and problems—all have real therapeuti
when the conditions in a classroom become tense or whe
om sets in. The depressed child can be lifted up; the disad
ed can live for awhile in fairyland; those with feelings o
uacy can overcome obstacles along with the heroes and giant

he quality of the life of the child may be affected by th
that he hears in the classroom. The stories of childhood ar
marked by poetic justice—the good are rewarded, the evi
d. Wagner and Smith write, "The earlier such attributes a
kindness, generosity, fairplay and cleanliness can be em
and reinforced through storytelling the better." [2] Childrer
nade aware of the advantages that come from telling th
king turns, and recognizing the differences between "thin
e." This awareness, of course, does not usually find expres
nmediate changes in behavior; it is one more step up th
er of socialization.

erature can be chosen for its own sake. If it links up with
t class interest in travel, geography, stars, seasons, and
, so much the better." [3] It is likely that storytelling wil
nd expand knowledge and interest in other subjects. I
rve to upgrade the child's taste in literature, to whet hi
r reading on his own, and to direct and diversify hi
erest.

vorld permeated with noise, bombarded with verbalism
tions, a child learns early, in self-defense, to "tune out."
must then use methods designed to develop effective
lls. Listening to stories provides wonderful opportuni-
development. He is almost always willing to lister
nd in doing so he learns to listen for:

main ideas in the story.

Anthony Wagner and Robert W. Smith, Teacher's Guide to Story-
e, Iowa: Wm. C. Brown Company, Publishers, 1958), p. 2.
K. Trauger, Language Arts in Elementary Schools (New York:
ok Company, Inc., 1963), p. 235.

evoke expressions of horror and exclamations epitomized by "Those deadly things!" Those required and restrictive written reports are a strange contradiction in American education. In effect, many teachers attempt to develop love for reading and appreciation for literature through a process which is thoroughly hated and despised.

The insistence on the formal, written report as evidence of reading is not only unwise; it is unnecessary! The time spent by the children in writing the reports can be much more profitably spent in the development of oral language skills; the time used by the teacher in grading them would be more rewarding if used for personal reading or other recreation. There are many, many ways to check on individual reading. The following may be more interesting, more stimulating, and better designed to motivate reading.

1. A simulated interview with the author: One or more "newspaper reporters" may quiz the "author" about his new book. This technique has the advantage of requiring added research and of devising interesting questions.

2. A speech by the author: A child who has read several publications by the same author may prepare a talk to be presented at a writers' convention. He should talk about sources of ideas, the locale for his stories, and likenesses and differences in plot and characters.

3. A "Meet the Press" conference: This is the same as the first except that the entire class may be involved in the questioning procedures.

4. Panel discussions: Small groups of children may participate in discussions of:

   a. Books of the same type, such as mysteries, family life, animal stories, or science areas.

   b. The series of books which have always been so dear to the hearts of so many child readers.

   c. Books by the same author.

   d. Anthologies and poetry or folklore.

5. Debate-type discussions: Two or four children may discuss a book on the "I like–I don't like" basis. This procedure is highly productive of further reading because the listeners take sides and read the controversial books.

6. Arts and crafts activities. Individuals or small groups may do such things as:

a. Make a roller movie and tell the story as it "rolls." A scene for each chapter will allow each child in a group to have a turn.

b. Make peep shows of scenes from one book or from several. This is a wonderful activity to share with other classes or with adult visitors.

c. Draw a single illustration and explain how this incident fits into the plot.

d. Draw a series of illustrations or a comic strip or even a comic book to explain the story.

e. Set up a bulletin board or sections of bulletin boards. Ideas from stories may be presented and the titles posted as the viewers guess them.

7. Creative play activities. The pupils may work in groups to prepare such dramatic presentations as:

a. Puppet plays of stories or episodes from stories.

b. Pantomimes of outstanding characters and events.

c. Dramatizations of adaptations of the story.

8. Answer roll call with "thumbnail" book reviews. If the class is too large to allow everyone to respond during one period, certain natural groupings such as boys or girls or reading groups may be used.

9. Play a "guess who" game: Divide the class into teams. One group member describes a character; someone from the other team must name the character, book, and author. This is especially appropriate for groups in which certain books are very popular and are passed from one child to another.

10. Book sharing in reading groups: Many books can be reviewed if the entire reading period is set aside for all groups to meet simultaneously. Each group may be allowed to choose one review to be presented to the entire class. Or each group may be asked to think of some interesting way to present the best book to the class.

These suggestions are just a small sampling of the many ways of book reporting which creative teachers and children can devise. It is hoped that such procedures will make reporting on books as stimulating and interesting as reading books. Perhaps the next generation will have a different and more positive reaction from the usual hatred of book reports which is such a frequent response to them today.

Story time is instructional time

Blessed is the storyteller and fortuna[...] the multiple learnings from storytelling occu[...] setting imaginable. Stories have been used [...] since the dawn of time. Folklore has been [...] of society. The bards and minstrels of anc[...] the history, values, and standards of the [...] The grannies who told stories and san[...] young that they, too, could be heroes and [...] apply the magic formula of courage, w[...] telling remains one of the most versatil[...]

Those who try it are inevitably [...] telling is remarkably easy; it requires [...] equipment. It is unfortunate that som[...] production of telling stories. The fa[...] teacher can learn to tell a simple st[...] If she learns even one a month, sh[...] repertoire, and, of course, her chil[...] over and over again. This writer ha[...] ers into classrooms to tell stories w[...] difficulty is getting them to stop t[...] it is over. With great enthusiasm[...] "It was just great! The childre[...] thought I wanted to be a teacher[...]

values and advantages

The educational values [...] trum of the skills, understand[...] cluded in the elementary cur[...] are almost as pervasive. No [...] so much to establish the kin[...] ships which are so importan[...] tells you a story likes you! [...] telling act implies sensitivi[...] their ability to listen and [...] ment and reactions.

is a [...]
tance [...]
coura[...]
ident[...]
value[...]
bored[...]
vanta[...]
inade[...]
killers.[...]

stories [...]
usually [...]
punishe[...]
honesty[...]
bedded [...]
can be [...]
truth, ta[...]
and min[...]
sion in i[...]
long lad[...]

"Li[...]
the curre[...]
daily new[...]
link up a[...]
will also s[...]
appetite f[...]
reading in[...]

In a [...]
and exhort[...]
The teache[...]
listening sk[...]
ties for thi[...]
attentively, [...]

1. The[...]

2 Joseph [...]
telling (Dubuqu[...]
3 Wilmer [...]
McGraw-Hill B[...]

2. The substantiating ideas or data.
3. The sequence of events.
4. Vivid, descriptive words and sentences.
5. Precise language.
6. Story elements: introduction, body, and climax.
7. Consistency and cause-and-effect relationships.

As he listens he is also learning the skills of oral communication. Frequently, the story content will make him eager to relate his own experiences. Now, he can put those skills to work! He has something to talk about; he is better able to organize his experience in a sequential pattern; he can order his thoughts along a story line; his sentence structure has become more complex; and his vocabulary has increased to a point of adequacy. This utopian situation doesn't occur as a result of hearing one story, but each story he hears adds additional strength in verbalizing.

The quality of his speech may improve, too, for he is more likely to emulate the model of enunciation, rate, pitch, and volume provided by the storyteller than he is of the lecturer. He may never be a Carl Sandburg, but storytelling will help him become a more adequate speaker.

the qualities of the storyteller

The storyteller can strive to develop imagination, perception, insight, enthusiasm, spontaneity, concentration—these are the qualities of any creative artist. Add to these the desire to share experience with listeners, sensitivity to the needs and moods of those listeners, sincere joy in the sharing process, and you have the makings of a good storyteller. A person of such quality and integrity would never tell mediocre or unworthy stories.[4]

Good teachers always like their students. One suspects that the teacher who tells stories has a very special feeling for her children. This feeling may be a combination of traits made up of the ability to empathize, willingness to be a giver, and very deep respect for the emotional and intellectual reactions of others. A sensitive teacher is able to feel *with*, not just *for*, children. She is, in-

---

[4] Ruth Tooze, *Storytelling* (Englewood Cliffs, N.J.: Prentice-Hall, Inc., 1959), p. 31.

evitably, a giver, giving of herself, her knowledge, and her energies. She enjoys the reactions of the listeners; the sly grin, the shiver of anticipation, the wide-eyed wonder, and the delighted chuckle are evidences of interest and involvement. She seeks self-actualization for children rather than some unrealistic replication of adult behavior.

There are many things a teacher can do to develop a background of imagination, perception, and knowledge. She can study and read—history, philosophy, sociology, and anthropology as well as the wide fields of adult and children's literature. The more she knows, the better able she is to enrich her stories and to help children see relationships. She can expose herself to creative expressions in all the fine arts, for music, art, and drama are all related to man's attempts to interpret and enrich his life, and all have roots in folklore.

Wide reading usually results in richness of vocabulary and language usage. The good storyteller uses words as the artist uses color. The more precise and colorful the words, the more coherent and communicative the story. A large, expressive vocabulary will also help the teacher to develop her own unique style of language manipulation, and, thus, the storytelling experience becomes more satisfying to the teller and more rewarding to the hearers.

The human voice is a marvelous instrument that is too frequently unattended but never unnoticed! Teachers should realize that children are a captive audience, forced to hear the same voice over an extended period of time regardless of its pitch, volume, or quality. Storytelling time can be voice-improvement time, too, if the teacher is conscious of timing (tempo, rhythm, and pauses), the strength of sound (loudness or softness), and the quality of pitch (high, low, or squeaky). Listening to oneself on the tape recorder is often disconcerting, but it is invaluable to the teacher who wants to improve her speech.

The storyteller should be appropriately and attractively dressed. Extreme styles in dress or hair arrangement are distracting; the jangling of bracelets and earrings is disruptive. The children should be encouraged to remember the story, not the unusual attire of the teacher.

This same principle applies to the manner of presentation. A flair for the dramatic is fine. The use of facial expression, gestures, volume, and timing to emphasize a point, to heighten attention, or to create suspense is desirable. Exaggeration of any of these is most undesirable. The students will remember and talk about the histrionics of the storyteller, but the values of storytelling are lost.

Lest all of this seem to make storytelling more difficult than has been indicated earlier, it should be remembered that good teachers possess the attributes of the good storyteller. Buried forever, one hopes, is the stereotyped notion of the befuddled, beruffled, ineffectual teacher. In her place stands the vital, sensitive, well-groomed individual who is trained to make learning a stimulating, rewarding experience. Such a teacher will find storytelling a versatile tool of instruction.

choosing the story

The anthologies, books, and magazines are so full of good stories that choosing which ones to tell is not at all like looking for the proverbial needle in a haystack. Fortunately, there are only two major guidelines for the choice. First, the storyteller must like the story and feel that she will enjoy telling it. I recall an observation made of a lesson conducted by a very talented, enthusiastic student teacher. The reading lesson on this particular day was dreadfully dull: the teacher went through all the proper steps without a trace of her usual enthusiasm; the children were bored and restless. In reply to the supervisor's amazed inquiry, the student teacher blurted out, "I hate that story!" Further questioning revealed that she thought she had to teach it. "It was the next one in the book," she said. A teacher can't like all the stories in the books any more than she can like all the dresses on the rack. Arbuthnot takes a firm position on this when she writes:

> First, you must genuinely desire to tell your story. You must fall in love with the content or style or both. Never try to tell a story which barely interests you. . . . Of course, if you have not the emotional capacity to be deeply moved by these stories, then do not try to tell them, for there must be warmth and a loving appreciation in every word of a story if it is to touch an audience.[5]

[5] May Hill Arbuthnot, *Children and Books*, third edition (Chicago: Scott, Foresman and Company, 1964), pp. 382–383.

Second, choose a story that the children will like. This isn't difficult at all. If children love and respect the teacher, they will believe and value anything she tells them.

As one principal put it, "Listen, Miss Jones could put Davey Crockett on Paul Revere's horse, have him ride from Santa Monica to East Los Angeles carrying the 'Message to Garcia.' What's more her third grade youngsters wouldn't bat an eyelash." [6]

One caution: children dislike being *told* what to like. Adult critics decide that a piece of literature is a "classic," but the children decide *their* reactions to it, and no arbitrary label is likely to affect their opinions.

Knowing the growth and interest characteristics of the various age levels will assist the teacher in choosing books that children like. Stories with sensorimotor appeal are attractive to the four-, five-, and six-year-olds. They enjoy repetition and rhythm, so the accumulative tales such as "The Gingerbread Boy" and "The Old Woman and the Pig" are favorites. The little ones soon learn the familiar refrain; they love to repeat it with the storyteller, who, in turn, thoroughly enjoys the inevitable gasps of horror and giggles of delight. They accept talking animals and talking objects without difficulty as long as the concepts involved are related to their experiential backgrounds.

The next age group, the seven-, eight-, and nine-year-olds, might be called the "once-upon-a-time" age. Imagination runs high; creative endeavors are favored. Folktales, fairy stories, and tall tales are equal favorites. Because of their growing concern with fairness, honesty, and friendship, the pupils at third- and fourth-grade levels like stories in which virtue is rewarded and evil is punished. The ever-popular "Cinderella," "Rumpelstiltskin" and "Snow White" are built on this theme. These youngsters are developing a sense of humor, too, so this is a good time to introduce the shenanigans of the heroes in American folklore. The tales of Pecos Bill, Mike Fink, and Brer Rabbit are hilarious. Stories of animals are still favorites, and episodes involving children of these same ages are especially interesting. Selections from *Henry Huggins, Caddie Woodlawn, Call It Courage,* or *Door in the Wall* will find a ready audience.

[6] Wagner and Smith, *op. cit.,* p. 44.

The time of prepuberty is the age of hero worship. In their efforts to find adult models, the ten-, eleven-, and twelve-year-olds like stories depicting the bravery and courage of "real live people." Biography, history, and tales of heroes are rich sources of material. Stories of Roland, Robin Hood, Sir Galahad, and Joan of Arc have left vivid childhood impressions with many adults; good teachers will create these same memories for the present generation. The lives of Lou Gehrig, Babe Ruth, Jackie Robinson, and Babe Zacharias are stimulating stories for the sports-minded fifth and sixth graders. Anecdotes from *Tom Sawyer, Huckleberry Finn,* and *Penrod* provide the tales of daring adventure and dramatic action so appropriate to the almost-adolescents.

Whatever the age level of the listeners or the source of the material, the story which is successful must have certain characteristics. The plot may be developed through any of such diverse means as conflict, repetition, and contrast, but it must be cohesive, logical, and coherent. Even the events in a fairy tale must seem as if they would be possible if magical powers existed! The characters should be congruent with what the listener knows about his personality. The setting of the story should be authentic, easily established, and quite definitive about time and place. A distinctive style, rich in vocabulary and sensory appeal, with natural dialogue and appropriate sentence structure will help the storyteller convey the meaning. Finally, the story should "do something for" the listeners: explain life's riddles, develop understanding of human behavior, make the world more inviting and challenging, or tickle the "funny bone." There are literally hundreds of stories which meet these criteria. Choosing *the* one is an enjoyable experience.

preparing the story

Once the story is chosen, the task of learning it begins. Many adults can learn a simple tale almost as fast as it can be read. The trick lies in careful, interpretive reading. This involves more than literal knowledge of the story. Read the story to

1. Determine the tone or mood.
2. Determine the setting.
3. Note the descriptive words and phrases.

4. Visualize the "pictures."

5. Establish the sequence of events.

6. Recognize the climax.

7. "Hear" the repetitive rhythmic phrases, the refrains, and the unique "voices."

Then reread it to establish the flow, to piece it together into a smooth, cohesive unit.

To help you learn the story, Ruth Tooze suggests, you should decide which memory cues will help you the most:

> If you are a visual-minded person, you may see your story as a succession of pictures. If you are motor-minded—a succession of incidents. If you are audio-minded, you may hear the conversation and sounds that make such happenings come alive.[7]

Then rehearse the story—orally—to decide upon timing, gestures, and pitch. Memorization may interfere with the teller's feeling of oneness with the story. Memorize only the refrains and rhythmic phrases that help carry the action or the stories which depend on beauty of expression for the total effect. Many teachers prefer to read these stories reserving for telling those which can be made theirs.

The total process of preparation may be accomplished in thirty minutes to an hour. A more rewarding use of such a short period of time is difficult to find.

storytelling time

The values of storytelling are so numerous, the interest level so high, and the uses so diverse that anytime is telling time in the elementary classroom. Charlotte Huck writes:

> A teacher who has a ready stock of stories finds many opportunities to share them. While waiting for a film to be threaded in the projector, the teacher storyteller can utilize this talent. A rainy recess period can become a time of enjoyment rather than a teacher's headache. In addi-

---

[7] Tooze, *op. cit.*, p. 35.

tion to incidental storytelling, a teacher should plan time for this relaxing activity.[8]

Stories can be told, then, at any time that a period of quiet relaxation, a change of pace, is needed. Such times occur:

1. Before or after a recess period.
2. While waiting for lunchtime.
3. Following the after-lunch rest.
4. Between testing sessions.
5. As breaks between periods of concentrated study.

Stories should be told, also, in many situations and to accomplish many purposes in the ongoing instructional program. The values of storytelling as a planned language lesson were pointed out earlier in this chapter. As a motivational technique for the teaching of reading, storytelling is unsurpassed. Telling a story related in theme, plot, or characterization to the story for the reading lesson will create the highest level of interest. Many follow-up activities for the children leaving the reading circle may grow out of storytelling. One teacher told *Caps for Sale* to a second-grade circle. The group then read a story involving another peddler—the ice-cream man. When the children went back to the seats, they were to list the colors of the caps in *Caps for Sale* in order (to aid in understanding a sequence of ideas, and to develop listening skills), write a sentence or two to explain why the monkeys threw the caps to the ground (to help them comprehend cause-and-effect relationships), and draw a picture of the peddler wearing his caps or of one of the monkeys wearing the caps (to provide an opportunity for creative expression).

Storytelling can make significant contributions to the social studies program, too. The story of Jackie Robinson, the first Negro in major-league baseball, was told to introduce a discussion of the contributions of minority groups to American culture. Stories may also be used to introduce a unit, to motivate further reading on a topic, to explain a point or an event, or to culminate a unit of study.

[8] Charlotte S. Huck and Doris A. Young, *Children's Literature in the Elementary School* (New York: Holt, Rinehart and Winston, Inc., 1961), p. 386.

The physical setting for storytelling will vary from teacher to teacher and according to the purpose. Some teachers prefer to stand before the group; others like to sit in a chair in the midst of a circle of chairs. Standing has the advantages of mobility and visibility; sitting helps remove the status barrier and places the teller on the eye level of the listeners. For recreational periods children may be allowed to sit in chairs in a circle or, preferably, on the floor around the storyteller. This facilitates sharing of emotional involvement and identification. It seems wise to have children remain at their desks when stories are a planned part of an instructional period. This enables the learning experience to continue without the interruption of movement.

In all cases the children should be comfortable, the room well lighted and ventilated, and possible distractions anticipated and provided for. A word to the wise: no pencils, rulers, crayons, books, or papers on *any* desk! This, of course, is good teaching practice in all school situations requiring concentrated listening.

The author took a group of student teachers to a school to tell stories. The children had been told the circumstances of our visit. Afterward, one little boy approached in the hall, saying: "I wish Miss Weller could be my teacher next year; she would tell us lots o' stories and I like 'em and we could learn a lot, I betcha!"

He pretty well sums up the case for storytelling!

eight
Poetry and choral reading
world of words–and wonder

Poetry is magic! This description of a teaching–learning situation involving its use proves the point. A group of eighteen sixth-grade children from severely deprived homes sat in a semicircle around a visiting teacher. Fifteen teachers observed from their places on either side of the circle. This was a demonstration lesson, and neither the artificiality of the setting nor the intellectual and cultural status of the learners was conducive to effective communication. But the teacher chose to use poetry for the lesson, and her only materials were a good anthology and copies of certain poems for each child. She later confessed to having many misgivings about using this approach with children who had had very limited exposure to poetry.

Her reservations were certainly not apparent as she began with several tongue twisters. "Can you say 'Peter Piper picked a peck of pickled peppers?' " she asked. They could and did. "Why is it called a tongue twister?" The children answered. "Yes," she continued, "we get the words twisted because we don't say them distinctly. Let's try a hard one! Listen while I say it." The lesson continued with several of these. The teacher explained later that her purposes here were to establish rapport, to help the children to enunciate distinctly, and to encourage them to hear and pronounce the inflected endings *-ed, -ing, -s,* and *-es.*

Then she read "Mr. Nobody," an anonymously written poem

which is a perennial favorite of children. The pupils participated quite eagerly in a discussion of the identity of Mr. Nobody and of who might be doing the talking in the poem. She reread it with the children supplying the last line of each stanza. The use of this poem was designed to tie the subject matter of poetry to the experiences of the children.

The next poem was "The Grand Old Duke of York." It was used because of its strong rhythmic beat, the ease with which it may be memorized, and the possibilities for related physical movement. These sixth graders really became involved here. They beat the time with their forefingers and discovered the "silent beat"; they read the poem in unison and then in small group parts; they stood up, sat down, and sat "halfway up" as the words indicated.

Since the children were reacting so favorably, the teacher moved on to two more-difficult selections. She said that she would have continued with more of the simple rhythmic poems if the pupils had been less receptive and enthusiastic. The beautiful "Nancy Hanks" by Rosemary and Stephen Vincent Benét and "Mother to Son" by Langston Hughes were her choices. They were excellent! These children had some background knowledge of Abraham Lincoln; they knew about poverty, the "tacks" in life and the "bare places" on the floor, and they thoroughly enjoyed talking about them.

"What words would you use to describe these mothers?" was the teacher's next question. Vocabulary development was her objective. The children contributed several words which were listed on the blackboard. "I like these words. Do you know them?" she said as she wrote *tender, considerate,* and *loving.* They talked about these words. One boy said, "My big sister is considerate. She ironed my shirt this morning." (We learned later that he came from a motherless home.)

"Did Nancy Hanks's son 'get to town'? Did he 'get on'? What does the poet mean? What does it take to 'get on' in this world?" These sixth graders had a ball with these questions. Their responses spilled over as the children awaited their turns to talk about human characteristics and relationships.

The bell rang. The children shifted in their chairs, obviously reluctant to leave. One of the boys said, hopefully, "Let's do one more!"

His plea for "one more" sums up the universal need for emotional involvement in learning and points up two guiding principles concerning the use of poetry in the classroom.

In the first place, the natural language of childhood is poetic, filled with imagery and figurative expression. A four-year-old was delighted with the first snowfall: "It looks like whipped cream on the pudding!" An older child looked at the black smoke pouring from a stack and said, "The smoke is boiling mad today!" "I've got a full whole pocketful of cherries," bragged Sam as he joined his playmates.

Second, children come to school with a rich background of experience with poetic expression. Even those from the most deprived homes have chanted the nursery rhymes, the game jingles, and the jump-rope verses:

> Red Rover! Red Rover!
> Send Richard right over.
>
> Down in the meadow
> Where the green grass grows
> Sat little Susan,
> Sweet as a rose.
> She sang, she sang,
> She sang so sweet,
> Along came a fellow
> Kissed her on the cheek.
> How many times did he kiss her? One, two, three. . . .

Sometimes they make up their own rhythmic verses. Two three-year-olds on the seesaw chanted:

> Up! Down!
> Bump, Bump!
> Up! Down!
> Thump, Thump!

What, then, can account for the negative reactions to poetry which are shown so frequently? What factors become operant in the child's life to cause him to abandon his joy in rhyme and melody and to develop resistance and antipathy to all poetic expression?

The burden of guilt rests squarely on the ill-conceived teaching procedures which have characterized the use of poetry in the classroom for far too many generations.

Building the barriers

Unfortunately, many teachers teach as they were taught. Their thoughtless acceptance of outdated theory and their own resistant attitudes toward poetry cause the use of certain teaching techniques which serve only to perpetuate the fallacies. These approaches to teaching poetry may be facetiously categorized into four types:

The *didactic attitude* holds that poetry must teach a moral lesson. The effects are disastrous! Children are exposed to concepts too far removed from their own concerns and to abstract symbolism that is beyond their power of comprehension. Longfellow's

> Lives of great men all remind us
> We must make our lives sublime,
> And, departing, leave behind us
> Footsteps on the sands of time

may be meaningful to the mature adult; it is just so many singsong words to a child.

The *scientific attitude* revolves around the idea that educated people must be able to scan and analyze poetry. Poetry then becomes a workbook-type exercise, with the reluctant learners struggling to understand the intricacies of iambic pentameter, trochaic dimeter, the rhyme scheme of the Shakespearean sonnet, and the uses of countless literary devices. How unfortunate! The entire melodious movement is reduced to isolated syllables. Perhaps college English majors have some use for these kinds of information. Elementary-school children shouldn't even hear such terms unless a child's question indicates sufficient understanding to justify their use.

The *subject-matter attitude* restricts the use of poetry to that of informative devices in science and social studies. "Darius Green and His Flying Machine" is read not for its hilarious humor but

as a part of the unit on air transportation; Columbus Day is "cele-
brated" by reading "Sail On, Sail On"; the rumbling rhythm of
"Conestoga Wagons" is entirely missed when the poem is used for
information concerning the westward movement. Such use may be
justified, but only after certain attitudes and understandings concerning poetry have been thoroughly developed.

The *memory-trainer attitude* is apparently held by those who
subscribe to the ancient and discredited mind-training theory of
learning. An indelible school-days memory of mine concerns this
horrible business of the assignment of poems to be memorized.
Thirty-five sixth graders had to memorize and recite "The Charge
of the Light Brigade." Some got through the ordeal the first day;
the brighter ones waited and memorized it through hearing it over
and over; some never accomplished the feat, stumbling through
the poem time after time as the teacher supplied every other word.
The point is that every one of those thirty-five youngsters learned
to hate that poem, and the dislike no doubt generalized to include
all poetry. Required memorization is not only unwise, it is unnecessary. Children will automatically memorize the poems they
like as they hear and say them.

Teachers who operate under the erroneous assumptions that
underlie the attitudes just outlined would do well to leave poetry
out of the elementary curriculum and let more perceptive teachers
make up the deficit. The children who are privileged to have
teachers who have experienced the beauty of poetry and who have
discovered its multiple contributions to child development are
indeed fortunate.

Building the bridges

The appreciation of poetry and the ability to use it effectively
in the classroom are not part of some mystique mastered only by
the highly trained and inspired. The teacher need not be a literary
critic or an avid reader of Chaucer, Donne, or Keats. It's really
almost simple. She need only know and enjoy children and know
and appreciate poetry for children. A good beginning step is the
purchase of one of the many fine anthologies. Miriam Huber's

Story and Verse for Children,[1] May Hill Arbuthnot's *The Arbuthnot Anthology of Children's Literature,*[2] and *This Singing World*[3] by Louis Untermeyer are three excellent choices. A teacher will never make a better investment. The possession of a good general anthology will provide a lifetime of service and put a wide selection of stories and poems for every occasion at the teacher's fingertips.

The second step is the building of thorough familiarity with the world of verse for children. The only way to feel at home in this world is to read. Read widely from the poems suggested for the desired grade level and those concerned with interesting subject matter. The teacher who reads until she has accumulated a fund of favorites will then be able to match up the right poem with the right group or with the special occasion. And read *aloud!* Poetry, like music, is to be heard. There is no better way to develop appreciation and no better means of evaluating reading proficiency.

It is possible that teachers shy away from the use of poetry because of feelings of inadequacy in the reading situation. So the third step is the application of a few simple rules which will erase these feelings, bring the glow of self-satisfaction, and make listening a pleasant experience.

1. Read with a soft, natural voice—no "elocution," no histrionics. The appeal of poetry lies in the beauty of language and rhythm; it needs no theatrical additions.

2. Enunciate clearly and distinctly. Pay close attention to the inflected endings such as *-ed* and *-ing* and to the final consonant sounds such as *b, d, k, p,* and *t.*

3. Vary the rate of reading to suit the mood and the action. A uniform rate is appropriate to most selections, but, occasionally, acceleration or slowing down aids in the interpretation of some passages.

4. Experiment with changing the pitch of the voice to add emphasis. Use a low pitch to create suspense or to sustain deep emotion. A higher pitch conveys excitement, joy, and glee.

[1] (New York: The Macmillan Company, 1965.)
[2] (Chicago: Scott, Foresman and Company, 1961.)
[3] (New York: Harcourt, Brace and World, Inc., 1926.)

5. Maintain continuity of thought by careful attention to meaning. The end of a line of poetry is not necessarily the end of a thought. The reader must note this and carry the meaning to completion.

The teacher who would help her children enjoy poetry must choose their poetry wisely. Some general age-grade guidelines should be considered. Young children like poems with refrains, unusual sounds, and emphatic alliteration. They enjoy obvious humor, rollicking rhythm, and the element of secrecy or suspense. The here and now and the world of fantasy in simple, brief verses appeal to the primary-grade children.

Older children prefer the ballads and narrative poems which tell stories of adventure, mystery, and patriotism. Their humor may be more subtle; they can comprehend more abstract ideas, but they react negatively to long descriptive passages and to moralizing. Boys are especially resistant to sentimentality and ornate language. None of the "sissy" stuff for them! Vigorous action and strong beat are the poetic elements for the preadolescent males.

Fortunately, the choice of good poetry for children is made easier by the realization that boys and girls of all ages respond favorably to certain elements. Arbuthnot describes these in *Children and Books* [4] as the *singing quality,* the *melody* and *movement* of the word patterns and the lines, the *story element, nonsense* and *humor,* and the *sensory content.*

The final step in building the bridge to full enjoyment of poetry is an absolute necessity! The teacher must read it *to* the children with sincere enthusiasm and with full expectation that they will enjoy it. Don't say to children, "Did you like it?" Instead, say, "I *like* this line [or this thought]. Listen again!" or "I think this means _____. What do you think?" *Never* use poetry as a reading exercise. Children should never be asked to read poetry silently, and they should not read it orally until they have had much, much exposure to hearing it and many opportunities to develop adequate oral reading skills.

4 May Hill Arbuthnot, *Children and Books,* third edition (Chicago: Scott, Foresman and Company, 1964), pp. 197–198.

The principal emphasis . . . is on the teacher's rendition of poetry, and much less attention is given to reading by children since the oral reading of poetry is an especially intricate job of stressing meanings more than rhythm, of maintaining continuity when lines end in mid-thought, of modulating the voice to suit delicate shifts in mood.[5]

Opportunities and outcomes

Opportunities for reading poetry to children are as numerous as the minutes in the school day. Since the primary objective is the development of favorable atitudes toward poetry, the purpose of the initial exposure should be purely and simply enjoyment. In order for children to enjoy poetry they must understand it. So begin with poems related to their background of experience. After all, that is exactly what poetry is all about—a capsulized word picture of an emotional reaction to a real or a vicarious experience. Flora J. Arnstein puts it this way:

> Boiled down to its essence it is merely a reconstruction of an experience. And, here is the point, all poetry is just that: The presentation in words of experience either actual or imagined. . . .

> Even the youngest child is constantly involved in experiencing. Before he can speak he is feeling and either consciously or unconsciously recording and remembering experiences. So here is something we may build on—the child's own experience, the most necessary adjunct to his growth, indeed to his living. What we have to do is to relate his experience to that of other people and, in the matter of poetry, to that of the poet.[6]

For example, when children return to school the day after Easter, many will be wearing their new shoes. Read "Choosing Shoes" by Ffrida Wolfe. They can relate it to their own experiences, and this delightful little poem is likely to become a favorite.

[5] Henry A. Bamman, Mildred A Dawson, and Robert J. Whitehead, *Oral Interpretation of Children's Literature* (Dubuque, Iowa: William C. Brown Company, Publishers, 1964), p. 18.

[6] Flora J. Arnstein, *Poetry in the Elementary Classroom* (New York: Appleton-Century-Crofts, 1962), p. 2.

Choosing Shoes [7]

New shoes, new shoes,
 Red and pink and blue shoes.
Tell me, what would you choose,
 If they'd let us buy?

Buckle shoes, bow shoes,
 Pretty pointy-toe shoes,
Strappy, cappy low shoes;
 Let's have some to try.

Bright shoes, white shoes,
 Dandy-dance-by-night shoes,
Perhaps-a-little-tight shoes,
 Like some? So would I

But

Flat shoes, fat shoes,
 Stump-along-like-that shoes,
Wipe-them-on-the-mat shoes,
 That's the sort they'll buy.

The joys of Christmas give meaning to many poems; indeed, all holidays offer opportunities to read appropriate poetry—not as a lesson but as an enjoyable part of the general celebration.

All natural phenomena have provided subject matter for the poets. On a rainy day read John Ciardi's "Rain Sizes" [8] and "Galoshes" by Rhoda W. Bacmeister.[9]

Mark the change of seasons with poems; expand the trips to the seashore, the mountains, the cities. Read poems about the children's play activities and their homes, families, and living routines. One of the gratifying aspects of exploring the field of poetry for children is the happy discovery of its diversity of subjects, moods, language, and rhythm.

7 From Ffrida Wolfe, *The Very Thing* (London: Sidgwick & Jackson, Ltd., 1928). Reprinted by permission of the Author's Representatives and of the Publishers, SIDGWICK & JACKSON, LTD.

8 From John Ciardi, *The Reason for the Pelican* (New York: J. B. Lippincott Company, 1959).

9 From Rhoda W. Bacmeister, *Stories to Begin On* (New York: E. P. Dutton and Co., Inc., 1940).

Any time is the right time to read to children—as part of beginning or closing the day, during the quiet time after lunch, as a change of pace in the daily routine, as a stabilizer when emotional tension has been aroused, as a preparation for potentially demanding activities, while waiting for the call to lunch or the dismissal bell. These are frequently times of stress for teachers. Use them profitably and enjoyably with poetry.

After much reading for enjoyment and when the children begin asking for favorites there are many ways to expand the program. Poetry may be pantomimed or dramatized. One teacher used "The Merry-Go-Round" by Dorothy Baruch for creative dramatics. Read it—see how it gathers speed and then becomes slower and slower as the merry-go-round winds down. Her children saw the possibilities for dramatization immediately.

Merry-Go-Round [10]

I climbed up on the merry-go-round,
And it went round and round.
I climbed up on a big brown horse
And it went up and down.

Around and round
And up and down,
Around and round
And up and down.
I sat high up
On a big brown horse
And rode around
On the merry-go-round

And rode around
On the merry-go-round
I rode around
On the merry-go-round
Around
And round
And
Round.

[10] From Dorothy Baruch, *I Like Machinery* (New York: Harper & Row, 1933). Reprinted by permission of Bertha Klausner.

Poetry may provide the stimulus for a variety of creative activities. Children may illustrate a poem or draw a series of pictures based on a ballad. Creative stories are a natural follow-up to some poems, and many teachers are quite successful in having children write original poems. All of these activities provide meaningful opportunities for children to talk about their work.

Mature readers will enjoy planning and participating in a poetry-sharing period. In one classroom the students plan such a period about once a month. They decide which children will read, and sometimes, when the program has a unifying theme, children who have a favorite in the chosen area will volunteer. The readers have one or two occasions to practice with the tape recorder so that they can perfect their skills and feel comfortable when they read to the entire group.

Poetry can be correlated with subject matter very effectively if an adequate background of appreciation has been established. Teachers should maintain a continuing search for good poetry which is related to the instructional program, and children should be encouraged to participate, too. A poetry file, indexed by subject, will be a motivating influence and will keep the material readily available.

The reader may be wondering why a chapter on poetry with a great deal of emphasis on the desirability of the teacher's doing the reading is included in a book on the development of the oral communication skills. No other oral activity can offer children such a speech model in quite the same degree as hearing poetry read well. Children will not become more proficient in using language unless they hear beautiful language over and over again and internalize it. Nor can they talk well unless they have a rich store of concepts and understandings to give meaning and depth to their oral contributions. In the hands of a skilled, sensitive teacher the use of poetry will provide much valuable learning related to the development of proficiency in oral language. These include:

1. Lending importance to the child's own feelings and observations.
2. Broadening his base of experience.
3. Demonstrating the desirability of brevity and preciseness.
4. Providing exposure to colorful, beautiful language.

5. Showing the effectiveness of proper phrasing.

6. Setting an example of correct enunciation and pronunciation.

7. Providing a model of good qualities of pitch, volume, and rate.

8. Giving practice with worthwhile materials in oral reading.

9. Offering moments of unforgettable enjoyment and pleasure.

10. Lifting language horizons beyond the mundane and humdrum.

choral speaking

The use of choral speaking in the elementary classroom should be a natural and spontaneous outgrowth of the poetry read by the teacher. When children begin murmuring the words of their favorite poems as the teacher reads them, it's time to think about choral speaking—its structure, its requirements, and its purposes.

Choral speaking offers all the advantages of poetry and adds the power of socialization.

> The best reason for Choral Speaking in the Elementary School is that it will improve the every-day speech of children. It would seem that were reason enough to justify its use with young people, if one never were to think of it for any other purpose.
>
>   . . . .
>
> Bringing poetry back to the masses, from whence it came, is of course the finest attribute of the Choral Speaking movement. It is group interpretation of poetry instead of individual interpretation, although to be truly educational it should be group expression in which the individual retains his individualized powers. Through this group work a timid child will lose his timidity and gain self-confidence, while a bold child will learn to conform to the spirit of the group for best results.[11]

These are powerful reasons to make choral speaking an integral part of the language arts program. It should not be used as a gimmick to entertain or placate children or as a showpiece to exploit them but rather as a meaningful way to teach a multitude of speaking and reading skills.

[11] Carrie Rasmussen, *Choral Speaking for Speech Improvement* (Magnolia, Mass.: Expression Company, Publishers, 1953), pp. 13–14.

Begin with the simple rhythmic poems like the Mother Goose rhymes, Milne's "The Popcorn Man," [12] or Rasmussen's "I'm a Rabbit." [13] Move into the verses with a strong, catchy refrain like this one:

LEADER: A farmer went trotting upon his gray mare;
GROUP: Bumpety, bumpety, bump!
LEADER: With his daughter behind him so rosy and fair;
GROUP: Lumpety, lumpety, lump!

LEADER: A raven cried, "Croak!" and they all tumbled down,
GROUP: Bumpety, bumpety, bump!
LEADER: The mare broke her knees, and the farmer his crown,
GROUP: Lumpety, lumpety, lump!

LEADER: The mischievous raven flew laughing away,
GROUP: Bumpety, bumpety, bump!
LEADER: And vowed he would use them the same the next day,
GROUP: Lumpety, lumpety, lump!

The next step is the use of two-part poems. Try Stevenson's "The Swing" [14] or Beatrice Brown's "Jonathan Bing." [15] Let the children help plan the grouping and cast the solo parts as they progress to the more complicated poetry. The beauty and excitement of such poems as "Little Lamb" by William Blake [16] and "The Squaw Dance" by Lew Sarett [17] will be ample rewards for the time and effort. Finally, let older children work with such lovely literature as the "Twenty-Third Psalm," the "Twenty-First Psalm," or James Weldon Johnson's "The Creation." [18]

Those teachers who experience the satisfactions of such instructional procedures and children who are privileged to be in

[12] A. A. Milne, *The World of Christopher Robin*, illustrated by Ernest Shepard (New York: E. P. Dutton and Co., Inc., 1958).

[13] Rasmussen, *op. cit.*, p. 56.

[14] Robert Louis Stevenson, *A Child's Garden of Verses*, illustrated by Tasha Tudor (New York: Walck, 1947).

[15] Beatrice Curtis Brown, *Jonathan Bing and Other Verses* (New York: Oxford University Press, 1936).

[16] William Blake, *Works* (London: Oxford University Press, 1925).

[17] Alma Johnson Sarett (ed.), *Covenant with Earth* (Gainesville, Fla.: University of Florida Press, 1956).

[18] James Weldon Johnson, *God's Trombone* (New York: The Viking Press, Inc., 1927).

their classrooms will never classify poetry as "that sissy stuff" and close their eyes and ears to this world of wonder. They are quite likely to agree with Flora Arnstein who writes so persuasively:

> [There] exists a natural affinity between them and poetry. If this is true then it remains for us teachers to provide the setting in which such an affinity may be discovered and enjoyed by the children. It rests with us to throw open the doors, to provide the welcome and to play the gracious host, offering to share the bounty of poetry with our willing guests. Let us never be the ones to erect barriers to poetry enjoyment. Let us never be among those who strip children of their wings.[19]

[19] Arnstein, *op. cit.,* pp. 119–120.

nine

Evaluation

the summing-up

Teachers are generally progress-oriented. This is as it should be. The progress of the learner toward worthwhile goals is the product of education. This book has been based on the proposition that the development of oral language skills should be a fundamental purpose of the elementary school. These skills enable the child to become a more effective individual and a more capable member of a democratic society and to cope more efficiently with other learning tasks. Teaching techniques designed to provide many opportunities for the improvement of language usage have been discussed. The final consideration must be given to the evaluative process—to the formulation of specific objectives and to procedures for determining progress.

This is always a difficult business. It is especially complex in the language arts. The primary reason is that we have never really come to grips with the problem of specific expectations. As a result of this lack of specificity we too frequently "spin our wheels" in a morass of confusion and artificiality. In *The Cherokee Strip*, Marquis James defines this problem:

Grammar I wasn't obliged to give up, not having paid it any mind to begin with. I had no intention of doing so now. My position on grammar was that it served no useful purpose. This business of learning which words were verbs and which ones nouns; what was the subject of a sentence and what the predicate; and that mumbo-jumbo about moods and tenses—there seemed no more sense to it than learning the alphabet backwards (which one teacher required her kids to do). My teachers and my parents said grammar was necessary to know how to read and write properly. Bushwa! As often as any other kid, I was asked to read my composition before the class.[1]

Setting acceptable standards

The child comes to school with some established patterns of oral communication. These have developed from his interaction with his own unique environment. The impact of the schools' artificial treatment of language usage on his self-concept and his image of the significant people in his life can be devastating. If his efforts to communicate meet with criticism and rejection, he simply retreats to a more tenable position, reserving communicative powers for use in more acceptable situations. In this connection Martin Joos writes:

> Teachers must simply abandon the theory that usages differ in quality, as between good and bad, correct and incorrect, and instead build their methods and reconstruct their emotional reactions on the plain facts that are already known in part to their pupils. Teacher and pupil must come to terms with each other—and of course all the burden of coming to terms must rest upon the one who is supposed to be wiser and better informed—on the basis that usages can be learned without condemning those which they replace, that the learner has an indefeasible right to speak as he likes without school penalties, while the teacher has no rights in this respect but only the duty to demonstrate what uses are profitable in the adult world.[2]

The "plain facts," so well known to pupils and teachers, are that the *informal level* of language usage is perfectly acceptable in all communication situations except the most literary and that the school's insistence on the formal level is unrealistic and archaic.

[1] Marquis James, *The Cherokee Strip* (New York: The Viking Press, Inc., 1945), p. 120.
[2] Martin Joos, "Language and the School Child," in Janet A. Emig, James T. Fleming, and Helen M. Popp (eds.), *Language and Learning* (New York: Harcourt, Brace & World, Inc., 1966), p. 109.

The informal level may be defined as that which is commonly used and accepted by good writers and speakers and in the usual expression of educated people. It is characterized by such departures from formal usage as:

1. They invited Mary and *myself*.
2. It was *awfully* good of you to come.
3. I wish I *was* tall.
4. *Can* I be excused?
5. I don't know *if* I can attend.
6. *Who* are you looking for?

This is the standard recommended for the schools by the National Council of Teachers of English, the *English Journal,* and *Webster's Seventh New Collegiate Dictionary.* Elementary-school teachers would do well to think through the validity of their expectations and to concentrate their efforts to improve usage on the elimination of the gross errors which mark the illiterate level. It has been estimated that 40 percent of all errors occur in the usage of 15 common verbs: *do, go, give, see, come, sing, set, take, run, break, lie, write, begin, ring,* and *give.* We would be wiser to help children get over the "He done it" and "I seen it" hurdle than to spend time on such forms as "I am being critical, am I not?"

Establishing measurable objectives

Once the teacher has decided upon standards of language usage which are realistic and reasonable, she will want to translate them into specific objectives. During my years as a classroom teacher I spent countless hours working on objectives—for courses of study, for in-service meetings, for social studies units, and for daily and weekly lesson plans. Somehow my efforts seemed always to be wasted; the objectives never seemed to provide direction or to contribute to the progress of boys and girls.

The difficulties now seem obvious. The objectives lacked specificity, and they were not stated in terms that facilitated evaluation of progress. The following suggestions for establishing objectives for experiences in oral communication are aimed at overcoming these weaknesses.

1. *Think about objectives in terms of the pupil.* Learning does not occur unless there is some change in the learner. The traditional way of stating objectives in terms of what the teacher will do in the instructional process encourages the fallacy that the desired outcomes are automatically achieved when the explanation has been given or the material has been presented. We know that this is not true. The "lesson" may be taught quite capably and still not effect the desired learning. For example:

To teach proper enunciation of *-ing* and *-ed.*

versus

The pupil will show improvement in his enunciation of *-ing* and *-ed.*

The teacher may *tell* children about the common faults in the pronunciation of the suffixes and demonstrate how inflected words should be pronounced. Nothing has happened unless the pupils reflect their learning in improved enunciation. The emphasis must be on what happens to the pupil as a result of the teaching efforts.

2. *State objectives in terms of observable behavior.* When the learning experience is over, the teacher must have some way of knowing if the learning task has been accomplished. Some kind of overt behavioral change is the only basis for evaluation of learning outcomes. This is the reason that objectives which are stated in words such as *appreciates, understands,* and *knows* leave teachers at such a complete loss in evaluating progress. How can we know that the pupil "appreciates" or at what operational level his appreciation functions? Since we can't crawl inside his mind, our only basis for valid judgment must be the changes which occur in his behavior. The objective of "appreciation" must be reworded so that the teacher can tell exactly what the student who "appreciates" does, or says, or is able to do. For example:

The pupil *appreciates* good literature.

versus

The pupil *listens* attentively during story time.

The pupil *can relate* the events in sequential order.

The pupil *is able to discuss* the theme, plot, and style of the story.

The pupil *shows* increased interest in his personal reading.

Or, for another example:

The pupil *understands* the importance of having an adequate vocabulary.

versus

The pupil *uses* the new words in speaking and writing situations.

The pupil *keeps* his own word book.

The pupil *contributes* unusual, colorful words during vocabulary-building experiences.

If the learner actually exhibits the desired behaviors in functional situations, the teacher may be sure that he is progressing toward maturity in the skills, abilities, attitudes, and qualities she wants him to attain.

Evaluating progress

Obviously the desired outcomes in the development of oral language skills cannot be evaluated by any of the formalized testing procedures which are commonly used. Nor can we hold common standards for all the children we teach. This means that the progress of each individual learner must be evaluated in terms of his progress from his own individual status of language development toward the goals which he and the teacher accept as reasonable, challenging, and desirable.

The involvement of the learner in the process of evaluation is mandatory. He will progress only as far as he sees a need to progress; his own self-determined goals are the motivating source of learning. He should be encouraged to criticize his own tape recordings, to make notes of his weaknesses and errors, to keep and use a vocabulary notebook, and to practice oral contributions to class activities in front of a mirror. Teacher–pupil conferences are an excellent way to help the child identify his language problems and devise plans for improvement. Pairs of children practicing with each other promote self-evaluation, too. As the child listens to his partner and tries to help, he also identifies his own needs.

Some teachers are successful with group evaluation. If the emotional climate is one of mutual helpfulness and acceptance, constructive criticism from members of the class may point out individual and common weaknesses which need attention. There is, however, great need for caution in using this technique. The children who need the most help are usually those who are most sensitive to criticism, and they are not emotionally capable of sustaining critical comments from their peers.

Every teacher who embarks on a continuing program of oral language development must have some systematic way of evaluating and recording the progress of each child. The most effective way I know involves keeping a notebook or card file with a separate page or card for each child. One side of the page is reserved for the diagnosis of errors and weaknesses. Some teachers like to write a fairly comprehensive analysis of each child's developmental status at the beginning of the year and to write down other language needs as they are noticed. Such comments as these might appear in such notes:

1. Very limited vocabulary; uses practically no words outside those on the basic vocabulary lists.

2. Speaks in monosyllables; seldom uses a complete sentence.

3. Talks freely and happily about experiences on the playground but never contributes to class discussions.

4. Unusual facility with words; lacks depth in exploring ideas.

5. Uses compound and complex sentences frequently.

6. Speaks hesitantly and uses *and, well,* or *uh* to begin each sentence.

7. Uses past participle of verbs as past tense.

The other side of the page or card is used to comment on evidences of progress and to make notes on specific needs and plans. Parallel comments to those listed above might be:

1'. Used *crawly, wiggly,* and *black* to describe his caterpillar.

2'. Not much progress; one complete sentence in the committee report; try giving him a list of incomplete sentences to help him understand the need for complete sentences.

3'. Needs more actual experiences; spoke well when we talked about the trip to the fire station.

4'. Gave her several sources of information for her part on the panel discussion. Worked beautifully.

5'. Pair him with Tommy. Might help him to assume more responsibility and encourage Tommy to try more complex structure.

6'. The conference to criticize her tape was helpful. Work in another meeting to let her hear the improvement on the last one.

7'. Said "I done it" and immediately corrected himself. Slow progress but encouraging. Set up some oral "pattern" drills, requiring set responses to questions, such as, "Have you done your spelling?" "Yes, I have done my spelling."

A busy teacher cannot expect to write something about each child every day. Choose three or four for special attention each day and rotate around the class. Keep the entries brief, factual, and specific. In a short time a complete picture of each child's level of language usage and his particular needs will emerge. This is the basis for individualized instruction and for individual improvement.

Individual improvement has been the focus of this book. The learning activities and teaching techniques which have been described are aimed at providing for the sequential development of oral communication skills in the firm conviction that these will make for more effective personalities, better scholarship, and more efficient citizenship for the boys and girls of America.